Vegan:
The Ultimate Vegan Cookbook for Beginners

Easily Get Started With Over 70 Mouth-Watering Vegan Recipes

2nd Edition
By Jenny Walker

Table of Contents

Introduction

Chapter 1: Veganism 101
    Why Go Vegan?
    Health Benefits of Veganism

Chapter 2: What You Can Eat On A Vegan Diet and What To Avoid
    Read the Labels

Chapter 3: Vegan Breakfast Recipes
- TOFU BREAKFAST DELIGHT
- MORNING TORTILLAS
- IT'S A PARFAIT DAY
- CHICKPEAPPER CAKE
- A DIFFERENT KIND OF PORRIDGE
- LAS MIGANS
- DIY VEGAN HAZELNUT SPREAD
- FRIED BREKKIE POTATOES
- A BERRY BLUE OATMEAL WAFFLE
- MUFFINS WITH JELLY
- TOFUMELET
- BEAN-AVOCADO TOAST
- BANANA VEGAN BREAD
- VEGAN QUICHE
- WARM NUTTY CINNAMON QUINOA
- RAISIN RICE PUDDING

- VEGAN CREPES
- CHAI OVERNIGHT OATS
- PECAN MAPLE BREAKFAST MUFFINS
- YUMMY MEXICAN-STYLE BREAKFAST BURRITOS

Chapter 4: Vegan Lunch Recipes
- VEGAN SAUTE
- VEGAN BLACK BEAN BURGERS
- VEGETABLE SOY STIRFRY
- COCO SAUTE
- GREEN QUINOA CURRY
- VEGAN CASSEROLE
- SWEET POTATO BAKE
- VURRITO (VEGAN BURRITO) BOWL
- MUSHROOM PEPPERJITAS
- FAUX TUNA SALAD
- VEGAN-WICH
- CUCUMBER COUSCOUS SALAD
- ASIAN PEANUT QUINOA SALAD
- GARLIC CHICKPEA SOUP
- SWEET POTATO SALAD WITH A KICK

Chapter 5: Vegan Dinner Recipes
- SALAD CON MEXICO
- THE POPEYE SALAD
- FRUIT AND YOGURT SALAD
- CHILI TOPPED WITH PESTO
- MANGO VEGGIE SPICE SALAD

- AVOCADO CHICKPEA SANDWICH
- AVOCADO-BEAN CLUB SANDWICH
- PIZZUCHINIS
- THE GREEN CAPER LINGUINE
- ALMOND ROASTED PEPPER PASTA
- STEPHEN'S CURRIED EGGPLANT
- QUINOATATO SALAD
- THE ULTIMATE VEGGIE BURGER
- LENTIL SQUASH SOUP
- SLOPPY VEGAN JOES
- AUTHENTIC GERMAN POTATO PANCAKES
- SPICY CAJUN RICE AND BEANS
- DELICIOUS COBB SALAD WITH VEGAN HONEY MUSTARD
- SWEET AND SWEATY VEGAN CHILI
- EASY VEGAN PESTO PIZZA
- VEGAN-STYLE REUBEN
- DILL PICNIC-STYLE VEGAN POTATO SALAD
- FRESH MANGO AND CUCUMBER SALAD
- COUSCOUS STUFFED PEPPERS

Chapter 6: Vegan Desserts and Snacks Recipes

- CARROT CAKE
- VEGAN SWEET TREAT
- PETER PUMPKIN PARFAIT
- BASIL VINAIGRETTE FRUIT SALAD
- FROZEN PEANUT BUTTER FUDGE TREATS
- YOUR FAVORITE NON-DAIRY CHOCOLATE

PUDDING
- SANGRIA SHAVED ICE
- VEGAN COOKIE BITES
- VEGAN CUPCAKES
- OAT-CHIA COOKIES
- VEGAN GINGER COOKIES
- VEGAN CHOCOLATE COOKIES
- CHOCOLATE COCONUT ALMOND BARS
- MUSCLE POWER SEED BITES
- EASY-PEASY NO-BAKE CHOCOROONS
- PB&J ROLLS
- RASPBERRY BANANA SMOOTHIE
- SUMMER PEACH SORBET
- GRANDMA'S APPLE PIE ICE CREAM
- HOMEMADE STRAWBERRY CHIA JAM

Chapter 7: 4-Week Diet Plan to Get Started

Chapter 8: Last Tips For Beginners
16 Tips to Help you Transition to Vegan

Conclusion

BONUS GIFTS:
FREE BOOK CLUB ACCESS
FREE BONUS CHAPTER – High Protein Vegan Food Sources

Introduction

You've heard all the stories about how great being a vegan is; such as, how healthy it is, how energetic one feels after going vegan and how much better they feel by respecting nature in general. Yet despite its great reputation, many people are still turned off by it for many reasons, most of which have to do with the misguided beliefs they have it about veganism. One misguided belief, in particular, is that it is very hard to live a vegan lifestyle. For the most part, being unaware of how to prepare delicious and healthy vegan foods is the major stumbling block that most people have when trying to going vegan.

This book is about removing that stumbling block, as it features over 55 delicious vegan recipes you can prepare for breakfast, lunch, dinner and even desserts and snacks to help you rid your negative mentality about going vegan. After reading this book, and the recipes included, you will learn that changing your eating habits to vegan doesn't mean that you have to give up all the foods you like and it doesn't mean that you need to make huge sacrifices in your life just by changing your eating habits; but more than that, this book will also show you what veganism really is about. It will guide you as to what you should and shouldn't eat, it includes tips for beginners and even a sample diet plan; all of which are meant to help people like you who would like to start living vegan and want to know how you can do it as easily and effortlessly as possible.

So if you're ready to take the vegan adventure, turn the page and let's get started!

P.S. Make sure you read through the whole book, as there's a special bonus gift waiting for you at the end! Happy reading!

Chapter 1: Veganism 101

What is a vegan? Basically, a vegan is someone who doesn't eat meat or anything derived from animals such as milk, cooking oils derived from animal fat or eggs. Vegans and vegetarians are often confused one another, but is there really a difference? The answer is, yes.

A vegan is a vegetarian but not all vegetarians are vegans. A vegetarian can either be a vegan, ovo vegetarian or lacto vegetarian. Ovo vegetarians eat eggs, as well as plants, and lacto vegetarians tolerate milk consumption. Vegans are considered the "hardcore" vegetarians, as they do not, and will not, consume anything that is made from an animal, nor will they consume anything that is produced by an animal, such as eggs, milk, and dairy of any kind.

WHY GO VEGAN?

Many different people live the vegan lifestyle for many different reasons. Some do it primarily for health reasons, while others do it out of love and respect for animals and the environment. Some people do it for all three.

So what really is the essence of veganism? Most vegans would agree that these are:

- Harm No Sentient Beings:

    By sentient, we mean living organisms that have brains and nervous systems, making them capable of physical sensations and emotions. Basically, it means all animals and creatures of any kind. Veganism prohibits doing anything that will harm animals – it is that simple. Whether it is hunting, eating, conducting experiments, or testing on them with medicines and beauty products; these acts are a no-no in veganism. According to PETA, *People for the Ethical Treatment of Animals*, vegans save over 100 animals a year. Talk about compassion!

- Care for The Environment

By preventing the consumption of animal-based or derived products, the demand for industrial production of animals is lessened. This in turn reduces the need for precious resources like lands, fuel and water, as well as reducing the pollution to our natural resources like the air and water, among others.

- Help Solve World Hunger

The amount of grains and other crops that it takes to feed animals that are raised for meat purposes could feed dozens of people all over the world. Veganism is not just about compassion for animals, but also compassion for humans.

- Optimal Health

Numerous studies by reputable organizations and scientists have established that by nature, we are herbivores and as such, were designed to exist on plants rather than animal flesh. Such studies have also shown that plant-based diets substantially reduce the risks for serious medical conditions like diabetes, heart problems and cancers, among many others. Meat-based diets, on the other hand, have been established to significantly increase these health risks, as well as obesity. "Some people think the plant-based, whole-foods diet is extreme. Half a million people a year will have their chests opened up and a vein taken from their leg and sewn onto their coronary artery. Some people would call that extreme." - Dr. Caldwell Esselstyn

HEALTH BENEFITS OF VEGANISM

Since "health benefits" is such a broad statement, let's run down the health benefits of going vegan, shall we?

Abundance of Important Nutrients for Overall Health

There are many important nutrients that come from having a plant-based diet. It is rich in dietary fiber, magnesium, potassium, folate, antioxidants, ascorbic acid, Vitamins A and E, and phytochemicals. It is also low in bad or saturated fats that are linked to a variety of serious medical conditions, such as heart problems and cancer.

Lower Health Risks

Because it lacks the evil stuff and is rich in the good stuff (nutrients), a vegan lifestyle is one that can significantly lower your risks for major health conditions like heart attacks, clogged arteries, strokes, high blood pressures, diabetes, cancers, eye conditions (macular degeneration and cataracts), arthritis and inflammation. It also reduced the risks of slightly less serious conditions such as, constipation, halitosis, body odor, PMS for women, migraines and allergies. With so many health risks that can be reduced, it is a lifestyle that's really worth living. It is a win-win situation for the animals, Mother Earth and ourselves!

Sexier You

Healthy weight and body mass are one of veganism's best benefits, which obviously makes you physically sexier and more attractive. By looking healthier, you will feel better on the inside too, and your self-confidence will shine through. Living a vegan lifestyle also help you smell better, naturally, in terms of body odor and breath. Lastly, a vegan lifestyle can also lead to much healthier looking nails, hair, and skin, due to the added nutrients you are consuming through your diet. Sexiness overload!

Chapter 2: What You Can Eat On a Vegan Diet and What to Avoid

Given the definition of veganism in the earlier chapter, it is safe to say that a vegan diet prohibits eating anything that's made from the flesh of sentient beings (living animals and creatures that are capable of experiencing physical sensations and emotions) or any food items that are either derived from them, such as milk and eggs. Veganism also prohibits the consumption of products that contain ingredients that are made from animals, as well as their derivatives, such as animal oil or lard.

On the other hand, it is also very easy to learn what *can* be eaten with a vegan lifestyle; which is basically anything that's not made or derived from animals. It is that simple. As such, grains, fruits and vegetables are what forms the bulk of this vegan recipe book. I do want to point out that it is also very important to ensure you are eating vegan ingredients that are as fresh and natural as possible. Just because there's a "vegan" tofurkey sausage in the meat aisle at the grocery store, does not always mean that it is good for you. Some things products are still full of processed ingredients that are not natural or healthy for your body. So, just be careful and shop as fresh and local as possible.

READ THE LABELS

Going vegan means making label reading a habit. Why? It is because many foods that are commercially available in your grocery store may not look like they are made from animals or animal products; but, that doesn't mean that that it is true. For example, do you think you can eat just any ice cream if you're vegan? Consider that ice cream is a dairy product and dairy is derived from, you guessed it, cows - which are sentient beings. Even most protein powders are derived from dairy; that's why there are vegan protein powders made from soy or other plant-based ingredients.

Soon you will learn that food items that you once considered to be "healthy," really aren't that good for you after all. Granola bars are considered a healthy snack by many people; however, most are high in sugar and many are also prepared using oil that's derived from animal fat.

One tricky ingredient that many people don't keep an eye out for is gelatin. Gelatin is found in Jell-O, marshmallows, Starbursts and other candies. It seems harmless, but to a vegan or even a vegetarian, this ingredient is not tolerated. It is even used in some shampoos, face masks, and cleaning products. You may not have known that gelatin is made by boiling down the bones, skin, and ligaments of cows and pigs. Gross, right?

Now you know why reading labels are important for vegans. If you're in doubt after reading the label, better safe than cruel – don't buy or eat that food item. Instead of choosing candy or junk food, go natural instead and grab a banana, apple or other fruits and veggies for a quick snack.

Honestly, in this day and age, it's so common for people to be vegans and vegetarians, that there are many more options than there were 30 years ago. You'll find that most of the meals that you will make – you won't even realize they are vegan and super healthy for you! Your taste buds will adapt and you will soon crave fresh ingredients and savory spices. You will no longer feel tempted to have a bacon cheeseburger or a big steak. The longer you continue to eat vegan, you'll notice the change from "diet" to "lifestyle," and that is the ultimate goal.

Now that you've learned the basics of veganism and why you

will benefit from switching to a vegan way of life, it's time for you to get into the kitchen and learn how to prepare your vegan meals like a pro.

RECIPES

To help you see – and taste – the beautifully delicious life of veganism, I have prepared over 70 recipes that you can try out for yourself. That's what Chapters 3 to 6 will include. You will have fresh new ideas for delicious breakfasts, lunches, and dinners. There's also sides you can make and bring to picnics and dinner parties to ensure that there's a vegan option for you.

Then be sure to keep reading to the end for an example starter diet plan and also a BONUS chapter on how to get high-protein ingredients in your vegan diet!

NOTE: Feel free to research vegan alternatives to any of the ingredients in the following recipes, if you want to spice things up and make it your own. Just make sure you do the right research so that it is still vegan!

Chapter 3: Breakfast Recipes

1. TOFU BREAKFAST DELIGHT

Ingredients:

- 1 large clove of garlic, minced;
- 1 pack of drained tofu;
- 1 small onion, diced;
- 1 to 2 tablespoons of wheat-free soy sauce;
- 2 pieces tomatoes, already chopped;
- 2 tablespoons of water;
- Cumin, ½ teaspoon;
- Pepper for tasting; and
- Turmeric, ¼ teaspoon.

Directions:

1. Heat water and soy sauce together in pan.
2. Mix the garlic in followed by onions, turmeric and the cumin. Continue to sauté until tender.
3. Add the tofu and simmer for 6 minutes before adding tomatoes. Cook for another minute before enjoying with brown rice.

2. MORNING TORTILLAS

Ingredients:

- 1 onion, chopped;
- 1/2 pound of tofu that's firm, cubed;
- 2 cups of broccoli, chopped;
- 2 pieces bell peppers, chopped;
- 2 pieces tomatoes, chopped;
- 2 tablespoons of soy sauce; and
- 6 pieces of vegan tortillas (corn).

Directions:

1. Cut the tortillas in half before slicing into half-inch strips. Bake until crisp.
2. Sauté the strips in soy sauce until crispy. Stir often.
3. Mix in the onions and broccoli and cook for another 3 minutes.
4. Throw the tofu in and stir-cook for a couple of minutes more before eating.

3. IT'S A PARFAIT DAY

Ingredients:

For the first layer:

- -1 cup of strawberries, frozen;
- -1/4 cup of soy yogurt, preferably berry-flavored; and
- -Maple syrup, 1 tablespoon.

For layer 2:

- -Frozen peaches, 1 cup;
- -Maple syrup, 1 tablespoon; and
- -Soy yogurt, ½ cup.

For the parfait topping:

- -1 heaping spoon of raw nuts; and
- -Soy yogurt.

Directions:

1. Blend together all the ingredients for layer 1 and pour mixture in a glass.
2. Blend together all layer 2 ingredients and pour mixture in the same glass to top layer 1.
3. Freeze the parfait for an hour before topping with nuts and yogurt.

4. CHICKPEAPPER CAKE

Ingredients:

- Baking powder, 1/4 teaspoon;
- Black pepper, freshly ground, 1/8 teaspoon;
- Chickpea, garbanzo or besan flour, 1/2 cup;
- Garlic powder, 1/4 teaspoon;
- Green onion, chopped finely, 1/4 cup;
- Pepper flakes (if preferred), 1 pinch;
- Red pepper, chopped finely, 1/4 cup;
- Salt, 1/4 teaspoon; and
- Water, 2 tablespoons and ½ cup.

For Toppings:

- Avocado;
- Hummus; or
- Salsa.

Directions:

1. Set aside the vegetables after preparing them and preheat your skillet on medium heat.
2. Whisk together the chickpea flour, garlic powder, pepper flakes, pepper, salt, and baking powder in a small bowl. Add water when done.
3. Whisk well for 15 seconds to prevent clumps and air bubbles. Mix the veggies in.
4. Spray olive oil or nonstick cooking spray on your heated skillet to coat its surface. Pour all of your batter in the skillet for one big pancake and spread it out quickly and cook for up to 6 minutes per side. You'll know it is done

when you can effortlessly slip a spatula beneath the pancake and it doesn't break up when you flip it.

5. For smaller pancakes, pour less of the batter, dividing it into several portions.

5. A DIFFERENT KIND OF PORRIDGE

Ingredients:

- Almond milk, 1 1/2 cups;
- Brown sugar, 2 tablespoons;
- Cinnamon, ground, 1/4 teaspoon;
- Quinoa, 1/2 cup;
- Salt, 1 pinch;
- Vanilla extract (optional), 1 teaspoon; and
- Water, 1/2 cup.

Directions:

1. Heat your sauce pan on medium heat and measure in your quinoa. Season with cinnamon and cook for about 3 more minutes with frequent stirring or until quinoa is toasted.
2. Pour in the almond milk, vanilla and water followed by brown sugar and salt. Mix well. Once it boils, reduce heat to low and cook for 25 minutes or until your porridge becomes thick with tender grains.
3. If it dries up before being cooked, add some more water with occasional stirring to prevent burning.

6. LAS MIGANS (MIGAS FOR VEGANS)

Ingredients:

For the salsa ranchera:

- Canola oil, 2 tablespoons;
- Garlic, unpeeled, 2 large cloves;
- Large ripe tomatoes, 6 pieces;
- Salt, 1/2 teaspoon;
- Serrano or jalapeno chilies, 2 to 4 pieces;

For the vegan migas or veganigas:

- Canola oil, 1 teaspoon and 1 tablespoon divided;
- Chipotle chili, ground, 1/2 teaspoon or more for tasting;
- Corn tortillas, torn into strips, 3 pieces;
- Corn tortillas, warmed, 8 pieces;
- -Fresh cilantro, chopped, 1/4 cup;
- Non-dairy cheese, shredded, 1/2 cup;
- Plum tomatoes, diced, 2 pieces;
- Salt, 1/2 teaspoon;
- Scallions, trimmed and chopped, 4 pieces;
- Serrano or jalapeno chilies, diced finely and if less heat is desired, seeded;
- Soft tofu (water-packed preferably), a 14-ounce package; and
- -Turmeric, a pinch.

Directions:

For the Salsa Ranchera:

-Preheat your skillet before adding the tomatoes, chilies and garlic. Cook with occasional turning for 15 to 20 minutes or until charred, with the veggies' skins blistered. Remove as soon as the veggies become charred or browned. Allow to cool slightly before peeling the garlic, coring tomatoes and removing the peppers' stems. Puree the veggies with your blender.

-Heat the oil in the same pan over medium heat. Slowly pour in the veggie puree and season with some salt. Cook between 10 to 15 minutes or until the sauce thickens. Stir and scrape up the bits in the pan while you are cooking.

-When done, reserve one cup of the mixture and refrigerate the rest for future use.

For the Migas:

-Use a fine mesh sieve and drain the tofu.

-Heat the oil over medium heat in a medium-sized, nonstick skillet. Throw in the tortilla strips and stir/cook until golden and crispy, which can take between 7 to 10 minutes. Transfer to a plate when done.

-Pour the rest of your oil in the skillet and return to medium heat. When already hot, crumble in the tofu to make it resemble scrambled eggs.

Add in the turmeric and chilies for tasting. Mix in the ground chipotle and scallions. Use salt to season and stir-cook for about 4 to 6 minutes more. The tofu's water should have already evaporated but the tofu should remain tender like scrambled eggs.

-Mixed in the tortillas, tomatoes, cheese and cilantro.

Stir-cook for up to 2 minutes or until the cheese has melted. Divided into 4 similar-sized plates when done. Use a slotted spoon to keep liquids in the skillet.

Enjoy each serving with 1/4 cup of the salsa ranchera and the remaining warm tortillas.

7. DIY VEGAN HAZELNUT SPREAD

Ingredients:

- Cocoa powder, 2 tablespoons;
- Hazelnuts, skinned 1 ½ cups;
- Powdered sugar, ¾ cup;
- Soy powder, 2 tablespoons;
- Vanilla, ¼ teaspoon; and
- Vegetable oil; 1 to 2 tablespoons.

Directions:

1. Preheat your oven to 350 degrees Fahrenheit to toast the nuts for 20 minutes, tossing frequently to avoid burning.
2. While still hot, grind the nuts with a food processor, adding some oil and vanilla while doing so, to make nut butter. After making course nut butter, mix the soy powder in together with the cocoa powder and powdered sugar. If needed, add more oil. Blend some more until the consistency is as desired.
3. You can blend the nuts longer to make them smooth and thinner. Add more powdered sugar and shorten the blending process for a thicker consistency.

8. FRIED BREKKIE POTATOES

Ingredients:

- Black pepper, ground, 1/2 teaspoon;
- Garlic powder, 1/2 teaspoon;
- Large potatoes, peeled and cubed, 6 pieces;
- Olive oil, 1/3 cup;
- Paprika, 1/2 teaspoon; and
- Salt, 1 teaspoon.

Directions:

1. Heat the olive oil in large skillet on medium heat.
2. Cook the potatoes in with occasional stirring until they turn golden brown.
3. Use salt, pepper, paprika and garlic powder to season for taste before enjoying.

9. A BERRY BLUE OATMEAL WAFFLE

Ingredients:

- 1 cup white whole-wheat flour
- 1 tablespoon baking powder
- 1/2 teaspoon salt
- 1/4 teaspoon ground allspice
- 1 cup quick cooking oats
- 1/3 cup unsweetened applesauce
- 1 1/2 cups unsweetened almond milk (or your preferred non-dairy milk)
- 3 tablespoons pure maple syrup
- 2 tablespoons canola oil
- 1 teaspoon pure vanilla extract; and
- 1 1/2 cups frozen blueberries

Directions:

1. In a mixing bowl, sift the salt, baking powder, allspice and flour. Mix the oats in and create a hole in the center of the mixture.
2. Pour in the vanilla, maple syrup, oil, milk and applesauce into the center and stir until combined. Allow the remaining batter to rest for 5 minutes to thicken a bit.
3. Add in the frozen berries and cook the mixture in your waffle iron per the manufacturer's instructions. Don't forget to line the waffle iron with oil in between each waffle to prevent sticking.
4. After the waffles are cooked, serve and enjoy!

10. MUFFINS WITH JELLY

Ingredients:

- 1 1/2 cups all-purpose flour;
- 3/4 teaspoon baking powder;
- 1/2 teaspoon baking soda;
- 1/2 teaspoon ground nutmeg;
- 1/2 teaspoon fine salt;
- 1 cup plain soy or rice milk;
- 1 teaspoon cider vinegar;
- 2 tablespoons cornstarch;
- 3/4 cup plus 2 tablespoons granulated sugar;
- 1/3 cup vegetable oil;
- 2 teaspoons vanilla extract;
- 1/3 cup raspberry, strawberry, or grape jam or preserves; and
- Powdered sugar, for dusting.

Directions:

1. Preheat oven to 350 degrees Fahrenheit. Arrange a rack at the center.
2. Use paper liners to line a muffin pan with 12 wells. Put aside.
3. In a large bowl, sift together the baking powder, the flour, the nutmeg, the baking soda and salt. Create a hole in the mixture's center and put the mixture aside.
4. In a medium-sized bowl, whisk the cornstarch, soy or rice milk and vinegar together until cornstarch is fully dissolved. Pour mixture in the center hole of your flour mixture before stirring in the vanilla, oil and granulated sugar using a rubber spatula. Mix until no or only a few lumps remain.

5. Fill each muffin cup up to three quarters full with the batter and create a tiny indentation on each by spreading the batter slightly outward from the middle using a spoon. Fill each indentation with 1 heaping teaspoon of the preserve or jam.
6. Bake for about 23 minutes or until the muffins' tops become firm.
7. Allow the pan to cool for 5 minutes on a wire rack when done. Afterwards, take out the muffins from the pan to completely cool on the wire rack. Use powdered sugar for dusting prior to enjoying.

11. TOFUMELET

Ingredients:

- 6 ounces (1/2 package) extra-firm tofu;
- 1/3 cup soy milk (plus extra for batter consistency);
- 1 Tablespoon brown rice flour;
- 1 Tablespoon cornstarch;
- 1/8 teaspoon turmeric;
- 1/4 teaspoon seasoned salt; and
- 1 dash cayenne pepper.

Directions:

1. Drain all the liquid after removing tofu from package. Put them on stacked paper towels to dry. Press gently with additional towels to absorb excess liquid.
2. Slice your tofu into several pieces for blending.
3. Pulse all the ingredients together in your food processor or blender until smooth. Tilt your processors container to check if your batter will flow gradually. If not, put in extra soy milk measuring 1 tablespoon each until your batter becomes pourable.
4. Coat your non-stick frying pan with 1 tablespoon of olive oil and in it, cook your vegan "egg" batter over medium heat. Gently spread your batter to coat the bottom of the pan well. Cover the omelet and cook for up to 8 minutes or until its top looks dry already.
5. If you omelet doesn't move as you shake the pan, gently loosen it underneath using a spatula. At this point, you can add in your preferred vegan toppings on that part of the omelet that's farthest from the pan's handle. Slide the omelet gently onto your plate and when half of it is already there, tilt over your pan to fold the omelet in half. Allow to set for a minute before enjoying warm.

12. BEAN-AVOCADO TOAST

Ingredients:

- 2 slices sandwich bread;
- 1 cup homemade or store-bought vegan refried beans;
- 1 avocado, thinly sliced;
- A few slivers white onion; and
- Coarse sea salt

Directions:

1. Toast bread according to preference.
2. Mash the avocado and use it to top the toast together with refried beans.
3. Add a sprinkle of salt and some slivered onions to enjoy.

13. BANANA VEGAN BREAD

Ingredients:

- 2 medium bananas (2/3 cup) mashed well;
- 1/3 cup brewed black coffee;
- 3 tablespoons chia seeds mixed with 6 tablespoons water and stirred well;
- 1/2 cup vegan butter, very soft;
- 1/2 cup maple syrup or 1/2 cup brown sugar;
- 1 cup white flour + 1 cup wholemeal flour;
- 2 tsp. baking powder;
- 1/2 tsp. salt; and
- 1 tsp. Allspice;
- 1 tsp. cinnamon.

Directions:

1. Preheat your oven to 350 degrees Fahrenheit and line your loaf pan.
2. Mix the sugar and soft butter together until fluffy. Mix in the honey, stirring well.
3. Sift the rising agents, salt and flour, together then gently fold them in the wet mixture. Bake for up to 40 minutes or until your inserted skewer or knife comes out clean and the top turns brown.

14. VEGAN QUICHE

Ingredients:

For The Crust:

- 1 tablespoon ground flax + 3 tablespoons water, mixed together;
- 1 cup whole almonds, ground into flour;
- 1 cup gluten-free rolled oats or buckwheat oats, ground into flour;
- 1 teaspoon dried parsley;
- 1 teaspoon dried oregano;
- 1/2 tsp kosher salt;
- 1 tbsp coconut oil or olive oil;
- 1-2.5 tbsp water, as needed;

For The Quiche:

- 1 block (14-oz) firm tofu;
- 1 tablespoon coconut oil or olive oil;
- 1 leek or yellow onion, thinly sliced;
- 3 large garlic cloves, minced;
- 3 cups (8-oz) sliced cremini mushrooms;
- 1/2 cup fresh chives, finely chopped;
- 1/2 cup fresh basil leaves, finely chopped;
- 1/3 cup oil-packed sun-dried tomatoes, finely chopped;
- 1 cup baby spinach;
- 2 tbsp nutritional yeast;
- 1 teaspoon dried oregano;
- 3/4-1 teaspoon fine grain sea salt;
- Black pepper, to taste; and
- Red pepper flakes, to taste.

Directions:

-While preheating the oven to 350 degrees Fahrenheit, grease a round, 10-inch tart pan lightly. You can also use a 9-inch pie dish made of glass instead.

-Use a few paper towels to wrap your tofu, placing a couple of books on top to press the water out lightly while preparing the crust.

For The Crust:

-Whisk the water mixture and the flax together in a bowl and allow to gel up by setting it aside.

-Mix together the salt, parsley, oregano, out or buckwheat flour and almond meal in a large bowl.

-Mix in the oil and flax mixture, stirring until generally combined.

-Mix the remaining water in until its consistency is that of a cookie dough. It should stick together when pressed with fingers.

-Evenly crumble your dough on your tart pan's base. From the pan's center, evenly press the mixture into it and work outward and up the sides of the pan. Let the air escape by poking a few holes in the dough.

- Bake for up to 16 minutes at 350 degrees Fahrenheit or until firm and lightly golden. When done, allow to cool while preparing the filling. Increase oven temperature to 375 degrees Fahrenheit.

For The Filling:

-Divide your tofu into 4 pieces and process in a blender until creamy and smooth. If it fails to become creamy, add some almond milk to help while blending.

-Sauté the garlic and onion in oil over medium heat for several minutes. Mix in mushrooms and salt and continue cooking in medium-high heat for up to 12 minutes or until much of the water's been cooked off your mushrooms. Mix in the red pepper flakes, pepper, salt, oregano, yeast, spinach, tomatoes and herbs and continue cooking until spinach has wilted.

-Remove from heat and mix the processed tofu in thoroughly. Season if desired. Transfer to the baked crust and smooth out with a spoon.

-Bake at 375 degrees Fahrenheit uncovered for up to 37 minutes or until firm. Cool the quiche for up to 20 minutes before slicing for the best results.

-For leftovers, wrap and refrigerate for up to 4 days max. Simply reheat on a baking sheet at 350 degrees F for up to 20 minutes.

15. WARM NUTTY CINNAMON QUINOA

Ingredients:

- 1 cup organic 1% low fat milk;
- 1 cup water;
- 1 cup organic quinoa, rinsed;
- 2 cups fresh blackberries, organic preferred;
- 1/2 teaspoon ground cinnamon;
- 1/3 cup chopped pecans, toasted; and
- 4 teaspoons organic agave nectar.

Directions:

1. In a saucepan, mix the quinoa, water and milk. Boil in high heat. Then, simmer at medium-low heat with cover for 15 minutes or until much of the liquid is absorbed by the quinoa.
2. Remove from heat and set aside covered for 5 minutes.
3. Mix the cinnamon and blackberries in and enjoy 4 servings. Top with pecans and a teaspoon of agave nectar each.

16.   RAISIN RICE PUDDING

Ingredients:

- 1 cup water
- 3 cups cooked brown rice
- 1/2 cup raisins
- 1/4 cup maple syrup
- 1 cup soy milk
- 1/2 cup almonds (chopped and toasted)
- 1 teaspoon cinnamon
- 1/2 teaspoon cardamom

Directions:

Combine all ingredients in a saucepan and bring to a boil over medium-high heat.

Reduce heat immediately to low and allow to simmer. Stir frequently for about 5 to 10 minutes or until the pudding has thickened.

Pour into bowls and enjoy!

17.   VEGAN CREPES

Ingredients:

- 1/2 cup skim milk
- 2/3 cup water
- 1 cup all-purpose white flour
- 1 tablespoon granulated white sugar
- 1/4 cup butter (melted)
- 1 tablespoon vegetable oil
- 2 tablespoons vanilla extract
- 1/4 teaspoon salt

Directions:

1. Mix together milk, butter, water, and vanilla in a medium-sized mixing bowl and mix sugar, salt, and flour in a small mixing bowl.

2. Pour flour mixture into the milk mixture and whisk together until the batter is a smooth consistency. Refrigerate the batter, covered, for at least 2 hours.

3. Once the batter has been refrigerated for two hours, heat a medium-size frying pan or skillet over medium-high heat. Coat the warmed pan with a small amount of oil and pour in roughly 2 to 3 tablespoons of the batter.

4. Warm a medium skillet over medium-high heat. Coat pan with a small amount of vegetable oil and pour in about 2 tablespoons of crepe batter until it evenly and thinly coats the bottom of the pan.

5. Heat until the edges of the crepe are crispy and then flip the crepe to heat the other side until it is also golden and crispy.

6. Repeat process until all of the batter has been used.

7. Top crepes with fresh fruit, chocolate-hazelnut spread, or any topping of your choice.

18. CHAI OVERNIGHT OATS

Ingredients:

- 1 cup oats
- 1 cup almond-coconut milk
- 2 tablespoons chia seeds
- 1/4 teaspoon vanilla extract
- 2 tablespoons shredded coconut
- 1/4 teaspoon cardamom
- 1/4 teaspoon ground ginger
- 1/4 teaspoon nutmeg
- 1/4 teaspoon cinnamon

Directions:

1. In a bowl or Mason jar, combine oats, milk, chia, coconut, nutmeg, cinnamon, cardamom, vanilla extract, and ginger.

2. Place the lid on the Mason jar or cover the bowl with plastic wrap and refrigerate overnight or at least 8 hours.

19. PECAN MAPLE BREAKFAST MUFFINS

Ingredients:

- 3 tablespoons flax seed meal
- 9 tablespoons water
- 2 tablespoons coconut flour
- 1 1/4 cups all-purpose flour (gluten-free)
- 3 tablespoons pecans (chopped)
- 3 tablespoons coconut oil
- 1 teaspoon baking soda
- 1 teaspoon baking powder
- 1/4 teaspoon salt
- 1/2 cup maple syrup
- 1 teaspoon vanilla extract

Directions:

1. Preheat your oven to 350 degrees F and line 9 muffin cups with paper liners.
2. In a mixing bowl, stir together the flax seed meal and water and flax seed meal and set aside until it has thickened.

3. Combine both flours, coconut, pecans, salt, baking powder and baking soda in a large mixing bowl and whisk together until thoroughly mixed.

4. Add in the maple syrup, vanilla extract, coconut oil, and flax mixture.

5. Mix well until the batter is smooth and then spoon it into the previously prepared muffin cups.

6. Bake for about 15 minutes or until the tops of the muffin begin to brown.

7. Allow muffins to cool before removing them from the tin and serving.

20. YUMMY MEXICAN-STYLE BREAKFAST BURRITOS

Ingredients:

- 4 sliced white mushrooms
- 2 cloves of garlic
- ¼ cup diced red onion,
- ½ a red bell pepper, diced
- 1 package of crumbled firm tofu
- ½ teaspoon cumin; ½ teaspoon chili powder; ½ teaspoon salt; ½ teaspoon pepper; ½ teaspoon garlic powder; ½ teaspoon turmeric; all mixed with 3 teaspoons of water
- Tortilla wraps
- fresh lime juice (to taste)
- ½ cup refried beans
- pinch of lettuce
- ½ cup salsa
- 1 sliced avocado
- Pinch of fresh cilantro

Directions:

1. In a non-stick skillet or pan over medium-high heat, combine onion, red pepper, mushrooms, and garlic. Cook for about 5 to 8 minutes.

2. Then, add in the spice-water mixture into the pan, as well as the tofu, and stir together until the tofu has been cooked through.

3. Warm the refried beans in the microwave.

4. Add all ingredients into the wraps, fold, and enjoy.

Chapter 4: Lunch Recipes

1. VEGGIE SAUTÉ

Ingredients:

- 1 cup broccoli, very finely chopped;
- 1 cup cabbage, shredded;
- 1 cup carrots, shredded;
- 1 green bell pepper, chopped;
- 1 tablespoon regular soy sauce;
- 1 tomato, diced;
- 1/2 clove garlic, minced;
- 1/2 lbs. tofu, crumbled;
- 1/2 teaspoon chili powder;
- 1/4 teaspoon cayenne;
- 2 teaspoons cumin, ground; and
- 6 green onions, chopped finely.

Directions:

1. Sauté the tofu over medium heat with soy sauce until brown.
2. In another bowl, mix all the remaining ingredients well.
3. Toss the tofu in and mix well.

2. VEGAN BLACK BEAN BURGERS

Ingredients:

- 1 jalapeno pepper, minced;
- 1 onion;
- 1 tablespoon olive oil;
- 1/2 cup bread crumbs;
- 1/2 cup corn niblets;
- 1/2 cup whole-wheat flour;
- 1/2 red pepper, diced;
- 1/2 teaspoon salt;
- 1/2 teaspoon oregano, dried;
- 1/4 teaspoon cumin;
- 2 cloves garlic, minced;
- 2 cups of black beans, cooked and mashed;
- 2 tablespoons fresh parsley, minced; and
- 2 teaspoons chili powder.

Directions:

1. Sauté the garlic, jalapeno pepper, oregano and onions together in oil over medium-high heat until onions are translucent.
2. Add the red pepper and sauté for two more minutes or until tender. Set aside.
3. Mix together the veggie mix, breadcrumbs, chili, black beans, cumin, parsley and chili powder and make 5 patties from it.
4. Use flour to coat each patty on both sides before frying for 5 to 10 minutes on medium-high heat.

3. VEGETABLE SOY STIRFRY

Ingredients:

For The Vegetables:

- 1 tablespoon rice vinegar;
- 1 to 2 teaspoons coconut oil;
- 1/4 cabbage; -2 carrots; and
- 2 celery ribs.

For The Tofu:

- 1 tablespoon lemon juice;
- 1 teaspoon ginger;
- 1/2 block tofu, diced;
- 1/2 cup peas; and
- 1/2 tablespoon soy sauce.

Directions:

1. Shred all the veggies and toss with oil, lemon juice and vinegar.
2. In soy sauce, ginger, lemon juice and the tossed-veggies mixture, sauté the tofu and the peas until hot and tender.

4. COCO SAUTÉ

Ingredients:

- 1 cup broccoli, chopped;
- 1 lemon, juiced;
- 1 onion, sliced;
- 1 red bell pepper;
- 1 small carrot, chopped;
- 1 tablespoon tamari;
- 12 pieces of mushrooms, sliced;
- 15 ounces baby corn; and
- 2 cloves garlic, minced.

For the sauce:

- 1 cup coconut milk;
- 1 ginger, peeled and minced;
- 1/2 tablespoon tamari; and
- 2 tablespoons peanut butter.

Directions:

1. Sauté the garlic, lemon juice and tamari for up to 2 minutes before adding the chopped vegetables.
2. Cook, stirring frequently, until crunchy and done.
3. Combine all of the ingredients for the sauce and mix it with the cooked vegetables to coat well.
4. Enjoy with brown rice or as is.

5. GREEN QUINOA CURRY

Ingredients:

For The Roasted Cauliflower:

- Cauliflower, cut into bite-sized florets, 1 head;
- Cayenne pepper, ¼ teaspoon;
- Coconut oil, melted, 2 tablespoons; and
- Salt.

For The Curried Coconut Quinoa With Greens

- Apple cider vinegar, 1 tablespoon;
- Cardamom, ground, ½ teaspoon;
- Chopped chard, 4 cups;
- Coconut oil, melted, 2 teaspoons;
- Curry powder of choice (optional), ½ teaspoon;
- Ginger, ground, 1 teaspoon;
- Light coconut milk, a 14-ounce can;
- Medium-sized yellow onion, chopped, 1 piece;
- Quinoa, rinsed well in a fine mesh colander, 1 cup;
- Raisins, 1/3 cup;
- Salt, 1 teaspoon;
- Turmeric, ground, 1 teaspoon; and
- Water, ½ cup. Optional Garnishings:
- Green onions, chopped, 2 pieces; and
- Red pepper flakes, a sprinkle.

Directions:

1. Sprinkle salt and cayenne pepper on the cauliflower florets and roast them in the oven at 425 degrees Fahrenheit for up to 30 minutes. Turn over the florets

halfway through the roasting and continue until tender and golden at the edges.

2. Stir cook the onions for 5 minutes in coconut oil or until they're translucent. Add in the ginger, turmeric, curry powder and cardamom for another 3 minutes or until they smell good.

3. Mix the coconut oil, water, raisins and rinsed quinoa and cover. Upon boiling, reduce heat to simmer for 15 minutes more. Remove from heat and let the mixture rest for 5 minutes.

4. Fluff the quinoa with a fork and mix the greens, salt and vinegar in. Divide into 4 servings, each topped with the roasted florets. Garnish with red pepper flakes and green onions if desired.

6. VEGAN CASSEROLE

Ingredients:

- 2 cans Cherry tomatoes, peeled;
- Courgette, thickly sliced, 2 pieces;
- Cumin, ½ teaspoon;
- 1 tablespoon dried thyme;
- Fresh thyme, 2 sprigs;
- 3 cloves garlic, sliced;
- 1 package lentils, cooked;
- 2 Medium celery sticks, sliced finely;
- 3 Medium-sized carrots, sliced;
- Olive oil, 1 tablespoon;
- 1 Onion, finely chopped;
- 1 Red pepper, chopped;
- Smoked paprika, 1 teaspoon;
- 1 Vegetable stock cube; and
- 1 Yellow pepper, chopped.

Directions:

1. Gently cook onions for up to 10 minutes in oil or until soft.
2. Mix the spices, garlic, dried thyme, celery, peppers and carrots. Cook for 5 more minutes.
3. Mix in the stock, fresh thyme, courgettes and tomatoes. Cook for up to 25 minutes more.
4. Remove the sprigs of thyme and mix the lentils in. Stir and bring it back to a simmer.
5. Enjoy with quinoa or rice when done (optional).

7. SWEET POTATO BAKE

Ingredients:

- Canned chickpeas, drained and rinsed, a 15-ounce can
- Cinnamon, 1/2 teaspoon;
- Coriander, 1/2 teaspoon;
- Cumin, 1/2 teaspoon;
- 4 Medium-sized sweet potatoes;
- Olive oil, 1/2 tablespoon;
- Paprika, 1/2 teaspoon; and
- Salt (optional), a pinch.

For The Garlic Herb Sauce:

- Dried dill, 1 teaspoon;
- Fresh lemon juice, 1 tablespoon;
- Garlic, minced, 3 cloves;
- Hummus, 1/4 cup; and
- Water for thinning.

For The Optional Toppings:

- Cherry tomatoes, diced, 1/4 cup;
- Chili garlic sauce;
- Lemon juice, 2 tablespoons; and
- Parsley, minced, 1/4 cup.

Directions:

1. While lining a big baking sheet with foil, preheat the oven to 400 degrees Fahrenheit.
2. Cut the sweet potatoes in half lengthwise after scrubbing and rinsing them.
3. Toss the chickpeas together with olive oil and spices. Place them on the foil-lined baking sheet when done.

4. Rub down some olive oil on the potatoes then place them on the same baking sheet facing down.

5. Roast the potatoes and the chickpeas in your preheated oven for up to 25 minutes or until the potatoes become fork tender and the peas turn brown. When done, remove them from the oven.

6. While roasting, you can mix all of the ingredients of the garlic-herb sauce in a bowl by whisking them together. To make it pourable, add just enough water to thin it. Season further if you find the mixture lacking in taste.

7. For extras zing, add more garlic. For more savory flavors, add salt. For a stronger herb tastes, add dill. For a fresher taste, add lemon juice.

8. Eat the potatoes with the flesh side facing up and its insides a bit smashed down. Top them with the chickpeas, the optional parsley-tomato garnish and the herb garlic sauce.

8. VURRITO (VEGAN BURRITO) BOWL

Ingredients:

For The Brown Rice:

- Brown rice, rinsed, 1 cup;
- Cumin, ½ teaspoon;
- Curly kale, ribs removed, chopped into bite-sized pieces, 1 bunch;
- Jalapeño, seeded and finely chopped, ½ piece;
- Kale, lime-marinated; -Lime juice, ¼ cup;
- Olive oil, 2 tablespoons; and
- Salt, ¼ teaspoon.

For The Avocado Salsa Verde:

- Avocado, pitted and sliced into big chunks, 1 piece;
- Black beans, cooked, 4 cups;
- Cayenne pepper (optional), ¼ teaspoon;
- Chili powder, ¼ teaspoon;
- Fresh cilantro leaves, ½ cup;
- Garlic, pressed or minced, 3 cloves;
- Juice of 1 lime;
- Mild salsa verde or any good green salsa, ½ cup;
- Seasoned black beans;
- 1 Shallot, finely chopped;

For Garnishing:

- Cherry tomatoes, thinly sliced into rounds; and
- Optional hot sauce.

Directions:

1. After cooking the brown rice per producer's instructions, season it with at least 1/4 teaspoon salt for taste.
2. Prepare the kale salad by whisking together the lemon juice, chopped jalapenos, olive oil, cumin and salt. In a mixing bowl, marinate the kale with lime.
3. Make the avocado salsa verde by blending together well the avocado chunks cilantro, salsa verde and lime juice in a blender or food processor.
4. In a saucepan, sauté the shallots and garlic in a tablespoon of olive oil until fragrant. Mix in the cayenne pepper, beans and chili powder and cook for up to 10 minutes more or until the beans become soft and warm. If at any point the beans become dry, add some water.
5. When done, distribute the kale salad, rice and beans into 4 equal-sized servings and top each with a couple of spoons of the avocado salsa verde. You can garnish it with chopped cherry tomatoes if desired.

9. MUSHROOM PEPPERJITAS

Ingredients:

- A1 steak sauce, 1 teaspoon;
- 2 Bell peppers, de-seeded and sliced thinly;
- Cumin;
- 6 small Flour or corn tortillas;
- Garlic powder;
- 1 Jalapeño, de-seeded and sliced thinly;
- Juice of 1/2 lime;
- 1 Poblano pepper, de-seeded and sliced thinly;
- Portobello mushrooms, stems removed, wiped clean and thinly sliced, 2 large pieces or 4 baby pieces;
- Ripe avocados, 2 pieces;
- Salt; and
- 1 Yellow or white onion, thinly cut into rounds.

Optional:

- Cilantro;
- Fresh red onion;
- Hot sauce; and
- Salsa.

Directions:

1. Cook the peppers and onions in hot coconut oil, stirring frequently, until they turn soft and slightly caramelized. Season with salt, garlic powder and cumin. Set aside with cover when done.
2. Cook the mushroom in some coconut oil in a heated pan. Season with some salt and pour a dash of A1 sauce - vegan friendly of course - for additional flavors as soon as they turn brown and soft. Remove from heat when finished and set aside with cover.

3. Prepare the guacamole by putting avocados in a bowl and seasoning with a generous pinch of salt and the juice of half a lime. If desired, add fresh cilantro and onions.

4. Warm your tortillas in a microwave oven. Enjoy them together with your guacamole, peppers, mushrooms and onions. Optionally, you can top the warm tortillas with salsa and hot sauce.

10. VEGAN-WICH

Ingredients:

- 2 slices of whole-grain bread;
- 2 tablespoons hummus;
- 3 thin slices of cucumber;
- 2 thin slices of tomato;
- 3 slices of avocado;
- 1/4 cup alfalfa sprouts; and
- 1/4 cup grated carrots.

Directions:

1. Toast the bread and on each slice, spread a tablespoon of hummus.
2. Layer the vegetables and eat to your heart's delight.

11. FAUX TUNA SALAD

Ingredients:

- 1 cup raw almonds, soaked
- 1 finely chopped celery stalk
- 2 finely chopped green onions
- 1 minced garlic clove
- 3 tablespoons vegan mayo
- 1 teaspoon Dijon mustard
- 3 teaspoons fresh lemon juice
- 1/4 teaspoon sea salt
- Freshly ground black pepper

Directions:

1. After soaking almonds for several hours, rinse and drain them well.
2. In your food processor, add the almonds and blend until they reach a flakey consistency.
3. Add the chopped almonds into a medium-sized bowl along with the celery, garlic, green onion, Dijon mustard, mayo, and lemon juice.
4. Stir all the ingredients until well mixed and season with salt and pepper.
5. Serve in a wrap, sandwich or on a salad. Refrigerate leftovers.

12. CUCUMBER COUSCOUS SALAD

Ingredients:

- 1 cup couscous
- 1 cup finely chopped parsley
- ½ thinly sliced cucumber, cut lengthwise
- 1/2 shaved red onion
- Zest from 1 lemon
- Juice from 1 lemon
- 1 cup finely chopped cilantro
- 1/4 cup olive oil
- 1 tablespoon warmed honey
- 1/2 teaspoon chili powder
- 1/2 teaspoon ground cumin
- 3 tablespoon pine nuts, toasted
- Salt and pepper to taste

Directions:

1. Prepare couscous according to the package instructions and place in a large mixing bowl.

2. Add the cucumber, lemon zest, and red onion into the couscous bowl, along with the chopped herbs.

3. In a separate bowl, combine olive oil, honey, cumin, lemon juice, and chili powder together and whisk until well-blended. Pour over and mix into the couscous.

4. Add in the pine nuts and pepper and salt to taste.

5. Serve right away or refrigerate for later. Cover and refrigerate leftovers for no longer than 5 days.

13. ASIAN PEANUT QUINOA SALAD

Ingredients:

- 1 teaspoon oil
- ⅓ cup dry quinoa
- 2 cucumbers
- 1 peeled large carrot
- 1 cup edamame, shelled
- ¼ cup sliced green onions
- 3 tablespoons peanut butter
- 1½ tablespoons soy sauce
- 1 clove garlic, minced
- 1 teaspoon rice wine vinegar
- 1 teaspoon agave nectar
- 1 tablespoon sesame oil
- 1 tablespoon olive oil
- ¼ teaspoon salt
- Black pepper

Directions:

1. Prepare quinoa according to the package instructions and place in a large bowl.

2. Julienne or spiralize the carrots and cucumbers and set aside in a large bowl.

3. Combine the edamame, green onions, and quinoa into the vegetable bowl and toss together.

4. Combine remaining unused ingredients into a food processor to create the salad dressing. Blend until

smooth and pour liberally over the vegetable/quinoa mixture.

5. Serve and enjoy.

14. GARLIC CHICKPEA SOUP

Ingredients:

- 3 (15 ounce) cans drained and rinsed chickpeas
- 8 thinly sliced cloves of garlic
- 6 tablespoons olive oil, divided
- 1 tablespoon minced fresh thyme leaves
- 1/2 teaspoon red pepper flakes
- 4 cups vegetable broth
- Sherry vinegar
- Kosher salt

Directions:

- In a sauté pan, combine the garlic, red pepper flakes, thyme and 3 tablespoons of the olive oil and cook over medium heat. Stir occasionally and then add in the chickpeas. Stir for 2 more minutes.

- Add in the vegetable broth and bring to a boil. Reduce the heat and allow to simmer for about 25 minutes.

- Add in the remaining olive oil and transfer to a food processor or blender. Mix well until the mixture is smooth, but not too runny.

- Season with the salt and vinegar to your liking.

- Spoon into a bowl and garnish with a little olive oil and red pepper flakes.

15. SWEET POTATO SALAD WITH A KICK

Ingredients:

- 4 large sweet potatoes, peeled and cubed
- 1/4 cup red-wine vinegar
- 1/2 cup extra-virgin olive oil, divided
- 1 medium red bell pepper
- 2 teaspoons cumin
- 1/2 cup minced fresh mint leaves
- 1/2 cup sliced scallion
- 1 fresh minced jalapeño pepper
- Salt and black pepper

Directions:

1. Preheat your oven to 400 degrees Fahrenheit and place cubed potatoes on a baking sheet. Pour 2 tablespoons of olive oil over the potatoes and turn them to coat.

2. Add a pinch of salt and pepper over the potatoes and roast for about 30 minutes, or until brown on the outside. Remove from oven and set aside.

3. In a food processor or blender, combine the remaining olive oil, vinegar, cumin, salt and pepper, and seeded bell pepper. Puree the mixture until completely smooth and blended.

4. Mix the potatoes with the jalapenos, scallions, and mint leaves and coat with at least a ½ cup of dressing.

5. Add more dressing if needed and serve right away.

Chapter 5: Dinner Recipes

1. SALAD CON MEXICO

Ingredients:

- 1 avocado, cubed;
- 16 ounces salsa;
- 2 cups corn;
- 3 cups black or pinto beans, cooked;
- 3 cups sorghum, cooked; and
- Salt to taste.

Directions:

1. Mix all of the ingredients together in a big bowl, except for your avocado.
2. When done, mix in the chopped avocado and gently stir to blend generously throughout the mixture.
3. Since this is best enjoyed cold, leave the salad in the fridge for at least 1 hour before enjoying.

2. THE POPEYE SALAD

Ingredients:

- 1 medium-sized carrot, shredded;
- 1 tablespoon balsamic vinegar;
- 1/2 bell pepper;
- 1/2 cup broccoli, cooked;
- 1/2 cup cabbage, shredded;
- 1/2 cup tomato, chopped;
- 2 cups spinach, chopped; and

- Pepper and salt to taste.

Directions:

1. Simply toss all ingredients together! Easy as that!

3. FRUIT AND YOGURT SALAD

Ingredients:

- 1 cup apple, chopped;
- 1 cup blueberries;
- 1 cup grapes;
- 1 cup orange, chopped;
- 1 cup soy yogurt;
- 1 cup strawberries, chopped;
- 1/4 cup almonds, chopped;
- 1/4 cup coconut, shredded; and
- 2 pieces kiwi fruit.

Directions:

1. In a medium-size bowl, mix everything together except for the yogurt.
2. Mix the soy yogurt in until distributed evenly.
3. Eat immediately or refrigerate for later.

4. CHILI TOPPED WITH PESTO

Ingredients:

- Extra-virgin olive oil, 1 tablespoon + 1/4 cup;
- Yellow onion, chopped, 1 small piece;
- Carrots, diced, 2 pieces;
- Diced tomatoes with liquids, a 14.5-ounce can;
- Salt;
- Black pepper;
- Chickpeas, rinsed and drained, a 15.5-ounce can;
- Cannellini beans, rinsed and drained, a 15.5-ounce can;
- Kidney beans, rinsed and drained, a 15.5-ounce can;
- Garlic, finely chopped, 1 clove;
- Pine nuts, chopped, 3 tablespoons; and
- Fresh flat-leaf parsley, chopped, 1 cup.

Directions:

1. Cook the carrots and onions in a tablespoon of oil for 5 minutes or until they become tender.
2. Still in liquid, mix in the tomatoes together with 1 ½ teaspoons of salt, ½ teaspoon of pepper and 2 cups water. Upon boiling, add the kidney beans, chickpeas and cannellini beans and cook for about 3 minutes more or until hot.
3. Mix together the remaining ¼ cup of olive oil, garlic, parsley, pine nuts, 1/8 teaspoon of pepper and 1/4 teaspoon of salt for the pesto mixture.
4. Divide the chili into 4 portions, each topped with your pesto mixture.

5. MANGO VEGGIE SPICE SALAD

Ingredients:

- Chili powder, divided, 2 1/2 teaspoons;
- Cooked lentils, rinsed, a 15-ounce can;
- Curry powder, divided, 2 1/2 teaspoons;
- 2 Eggplants, trimmed and cut into 1-inch cubes;
- Fresh cilantro, chopped, 1/4 cup;
- Honey, 1/4 cup;
- Lemon or lime juice, 1/3 cup (or more if desired);
- Olive oil, divided, 4 tablespoons;
- Pepper, freshly ground, 1/4 teaspoon or more to taste;
- Prepared salsa, 1/4 cup;
- 2 Ripe mangoes, peeled and diced;
- Roasted peanuts, coarsely chopped, 1/4 cup;
- Romaine lettuce, torn, 4 cups;
- Salt, 1/4 teaspoon; and
- Scallions, coarsely chopped, 2 bunches

Directions:

1. In a big bowl, mix together the 2 teaspoons of chili powder, 2 teaspoons of curry powder and 1 tablespoon of oil while preheating your oven to 500 degrees Fahrenheit. Throw the eggplants in and toss all the ingredients well.
2. When finished, distribute the eggplant on a big baking sheet that's ribbed. Roast the eggplant for 15 minutes in the oven, stirring once halfway through.
3. Mix together thoroughly the remaining 1/2 teaspoon of curry powder, 3 tablespoons of oil, ½ teaspoon of chili

powder, 1/3 cup of lemon or lime juice, honey, salsa, salt and pepper in a big bowl.

4. After roasting the eggplants, place them in a big bowl together with the scallions and lentils. Toss the ingredients together gently to combine.

5. Add more salt, pepper or lemon or lime juice for seasoning if desired. Enjoy it on top of romaine lettuce together with 2 tablespoons of mango, nuts, cilantro and scallions.

6. AVOCADO CHICKPEA SANDWICH

Ingredients:

- Any bread of your choice;
- Chickpeas, rinsed, drained, and skinned, a 15-oz. can;
- Fresh cilantro, chopped, 1/4 cup;
- Green onions, chopped, 2 tablespoons;
- Juice of 1 lime;
- 1 Large ripe avocado;
- Lettuce and tomatoes for topping;
- Pepper and salt to taste.

Directions:

- In a medium-sized bowl, smash the chickpeas and avocado together with a large fork or spoon.
- Throw in the cilantro, green onions and lime juice and mix well.
- Use salt and pepper to season the mixture. Spread on your favorite toppings like tomatoes and lettuce or on your choice of bread.

7. AVOCADO-BEAN CLUB SANDWICH

Ingredients:

- Alfalfa sprouts, 4 to 5 ounces;
- Avocados, pitted and sliced thinly;
- Black pepper, ¼ teaspoon;
- 1 Cucumber, de-seeded, peeled and sliced thinly;
- Extra-virgin olive oil, 2 tablespoons;
- Multi-grain bread, 12 slices;
- Salt, ½ teaspoon;
- Small red onion, sliced thinly, 1 small piece; and
- White beans, rinsed and drained, 2 cans (15 ounces each).

Directions:

1. In a medium-sized bowl, mix together the beans, salt, oil and pepper. Mash roughly with the back of your fork.
2. Divide the mixture equally among 8 slices of bread. Top each with cucumber, onions, avocado and sprouts.
3. Make 4 sandwiches by stacking together the open-faced sandwiches. The side with the avocados should be facing up and must be on top.
4. Finish each of the double decker sandwiches by topping off with the remaining 4 slices of bread.

8. PIZZUCHINIS

Ingredients:

- Diced carrots or pineapples for optional toppings;
- 2 Medium-sized zucchini, sliced;
- Pizza sauce, 1/4 cup; and
- Vegan cheese, shredded, 1/2 cup.

Directions:

1. Arrange the zucchini slices on top of a baking sheet while preheating the oven to 375 degrees Fahrenheit.
2. Top each of the slices with the sauce then sprinkle with vegan cheese.
3. Bake the zucchinis in the oven for up to 12 minutes before enjoying.

9. THE GREEN CAPER LINGUINE

Ingredients:

- 1 tablespoon olive oil;
- 2 cloves garlic, thinly sliced;
- 1/4 teaspoon crushed red pepper flakes;
- 12-ounces marinara sauce;
- 16.75-ounce jar Spanish olives, drained and roughly chopped;
- 13.5-ounce jar capers, drained and roughly chopped;
- 1/2cup fresh flat-leaf parsley, coarsely chopped;
- 1/2 teaspoon lemon zest; and
- 1 pound of linguine.

Directions:

1. Cook the crushed red pepper and garlic over medium heat for about 2 minutes or until they become fragrant.
2. Mix in the lemon zest, capers, parsley, and marinara sauce. Bring down heat to low and simmer for 15 minutes.
3. While simmering, cook the linguine per package instructions. Drain when done and mix in with the sauce. Toss to coat well before enjoying.

10. ALMOND ROASTED PEPPER PASTA

Ingredients:

- ¾ pound campanelle or penne;
- 4 red or orange bell peppers, seeded and cut into quarters;
- 3/4 cup pitted kalamata olives;
- 1/2 cup chopped roasted almonds;
- 1/4 cup olive oil;
- 1 tablespoon fresh thyme leaves; and
- Salt and black pepper.

Directions

1. Per package instructions, cook your pasta. Save 1/4 cup of its cooking water and drain the rest before returning the pasta to the pot.
2. Using your heated broiler, broil the peppers on a baking sheet, with the skin side facing up, for 8 to 10 minutes or until they turn black.
3. Remove charred skin from peppers using a paring knife. Clean peppers with paper towels and slice flesh into 1-inch pieces.
4. Combine the pasta with 1/4 teaspoon black pepper, 2 tablespoons of the reserved cooking water, 1/2 teaspoon of salt, thyme, almonds, oil, olives and peppers, tossing everything well. For a thinner sauce, add some more of the reserved cooking water.
5. Enjoy your pasta!

11. STEPHEN'S CURRIED EGGPLANT

Ingredients:

- 1 cup white rice;
- 1 tablespoon olive oil;
- 1 chopped onion;
- 1 eggplant, cut into small rounds;
- 2 pints cherry tomatoes, halved;
- 1 ½ teaspoons curry powder;
- 1 can of chickpeas;
- 1/2 cup fresh basil;
- Salt and black pepper to taste.

Directions:

1. In a medium saucepan, boil together 1/2 teaspoon of salt, 1 ½ cups of water and the rice. After simmering for 18 minutes, remove from heat and allow to stand for about 5 minutes with cover.
2. In the meantime, stir-cook the onions in oil over medium heat for up to 6 minutes or until soft.
3. Mix in the 1/4 teaspoon black pepper, curry powder, 1 teaspoon of salt, eggplant and tomatoes and continue cooking for about 2 more minutes.
4. Pour in 2 cups of water and allow to boil. Then, reduce heat and simmer, partially covered, for roughly 15 minutes or until the eggplant is soft.
5. Rinse the chickpeas and mix them in. Cook for 3 minutes or until heated through. Remove from heat and mix the basil in.
6. Top with veggies and enjoy!

12. QUINOATATO SALAD

Ingredients:

For the salad:

- 1 small, unpeeled, diced sweet potato;
- 1 tablespoon olive oil;
- 1/4 cup quinoa;
- 1/2 cup black beans;
- 1/4 diced red pepper;
- 2 cups spinach or kale;
- 1 tablespoon dried cranberries; and
- 1 tablespoon salted sunflower seeds.
- Salt and pepper to taste;

For the dressing:

- 1/4 cup mango, fresh or frozen;
- 1 tablespoon balsamic vinegar; and
- 1 1/2 tablespoons water.

Directions:

1. In a bowl, coat your sweet potatoes with oil and sprinkle some pepper and salt. Spread the potatoes on a baking pan evenly and roast in your oven at 400 degrees Fahrenheit for about 20 minutes or until the potatoes become soft. Stir the potatoes several times while roasting.
2. Boil the water together with quinoa in a covered pot on high heat. After boiling, bring down to a simmer and continue cooking for up to 20 minutes or just until the quinoa is tender and has soaked up the liquid.
3. Puree the water, mango and balsamic vinegar and set aside when done.

4. Let the quinoa and roasted sweet potatoes cool at room temperature.
5. Layer your salad in the jar starting with the black beans. Add the quinoa, then pour the mango-balsamic puree over it.
6. Put in the greens, diced red peppers, dried cranberries, roasted sweet potatoes and sunflower seeds before screwing the jar securely on top and placing it in the refrigerator.
7. Shake the jar well to mix up ingredients before enjoying.

13. THE ULTIMATE VEGGIE BURGER

Ingredients:

- 1 small baked sweet potato;
- 1/4 cup dry quinoa;
- 1/4 cup dry barley;
- 15-ounce can drained, rinsed chickpeas;
- 2 tablespoons parsley;
- 1 1/2 teaspoon cumin;
- 1/2 teaspoon salt;
- 1/2 teaspoon pepper;
- 2 tablespoons whole wheat flour;
- 2 tablespoons olive oil; and
- 1 1/2 fresh seeded and cored red peppers.

Directions:

1. Bake the sweet potato for up to 50 minutes in your oven at 400 degrees Fahrenheit or until soft. While baking, cook the barley and quinoa in separate pots each until both are soft.
2. Cut the whole red pepper into quarters and roast them in the oven for up to 20 minutes.
3. After the sweet potato has cooled post-baking, blend it together with 1 tablespoon of oil pepper, flour, salt, cumin, parsley and chickpeas
4. After both the quinoa and barley have been cooked and cooled down, mix them with the bean mixture in a separate bowl to make the patty mixture.
5. Flatten the patties using the back of a spoon to make burger patties 4 inches in diameter. Cook in oil over medium heat until both sides turn brown.
6. Enjoy on a bun with a few slices of roasted red pepper.

14. LENTIL SQUASH SOUP

Ingredients:

- 8 cups veggie broth;
- 1 chopped yellow onion;
- 2 cups rinsed red lentils;
- 3 sliced celery stalks;
- 3 large peeled and sliced carrots;
- 1 pound peeled and diced butternut squash;
- 2 cloves minced garlic; and
- 1/2 teaspoon nutmeg.

Directions:

1. Add all ingredients into a Crock-pot or slow cooker and make sure the lid is locked securely.
2. Set the Crock-Pot on the low setting and allow to cook for about 8 hours. If on high setting, cook for only 5 hours.
3. Serve and enjoy.

15. SLOPPY VEGAN JOES

Ingredients:

- 4 chopped scallions
- 2 finely chopped baby chiles
- 1 cup cooked lentils
- 1 cup finely chopped tomatoes
- 2 teaspoons tomato paste
- 1 red onion, chopped
- 2 tablespoons sweet chili sauce
- 1 tablespoon ketchup
- 1 tablespoon brown mustard
- 2 teaspoons apple cider vinegar
- 2 teaspoons dark brown sugar
- 1/4 teaspoon chili powder
- Olive Oil
- Salt, to taste

Directions:

1. In a saucepan or skillet, add olive oil and half the amount of scallions and cook over medium heat. Add in the baby chiles and cook for an additional 3 minutes.

2. Add in the lentils and the remaining ingredients and allow to simmer for about 20 minutes.

3. Remove from the stove and enjoy on a bun or bread of your choice!

16. AUTHENTIC GERMAN POTATO PANCAKES

Ingredients:

- ½ yellow or white onion
- 1 large potato
- 1/3 cup applesauce
- Egg substitute (1 egg equivalent)
- 1 tablespoon flour
- 1 tablespoon chopped parsley
- 1 tablespoon bread crumbs
- 1/4 teaspoon thyme
- Juice of 1 lemon
- Vegetable oil
- Salt and pepper, to taste

Directions:

1. Combine onion and potato in your food processor and process until grated consistency. Use a paper towel to remove as much liquid as you can from the potato/onion mixture.

2. In a mixing bowl, combine flour, bread crumbs, lemon juice, egg substitute, thyme, salt, and pepper and mix together. Add in the potato and onion mixture and continue to stir.

3. In a skillet over high heat, warm up a 1/2 cup of vegetable oil and spoon a 1/2 cup of the potato pancake mix into the pan. Flatten it down with a spatula and reduce the heat to medium. Warm for 5 minutes on one

side and flip and repeat until both sides are browned. Continue this process with all of the pancake mix.

4. Top the pancakes with applesauce before serving.

17. SPICY CAJUN RICE AND BEANS

Ingredients:

- 1 pound red kidney beans (prepare as per package instructions)
- 3 tablespoons vegan margarine (such as Earth Balance)
- 6 cups vegetable broth
- 1 diced large yellow or white onion
- 1 diced red bell pepper
- 5 diced celery ribs
- 2 minced cloves of garlic
- 1 teaspoon hot sauce
- 1 teaspoon cayenne pepper
- 1 teaspoon liquid smoke
- 1/2 teaspoon vegan Worcestershire sauce
- 1/2 teaspoon thyme
- 2 bay leaves
- White rice
- Salt, to taste

Directions:

1. Combine the margarine, onions, red bell pepper, and diced celery into a large pot and cook over medium-low heat until onions are cooked through.

2. Then, add in garlic and cook for about 2 minutes.

3. Add in the remaining ingredients, except for the rice, and bring to a boil. Reduce the heat to the lowest setting and allow to simmer for about 4 hours.

4. Serve over white rice and enjoy!

18. DELICIOUS COBB SALAD WITH VEGAN HONEY MUSTARD

Ingredients:

- 1 bag fresh spinach
- 1 cup halved grape tomatoes
- 1 avocado (pitted and sliced)
- 4 Tofu Eggs
- 1 package vegan bacon, cooked according to package instructions
- 1 package of crumbled vegan bleu cheese
- 1 can drained and rinsed chickpeas
- 1 can drained and rinsed black olives, sliced

For Salad Dressing:

- 1/2 cup vegan mayonnaise
- 4 tablespoons yellow mustard
- 3 tablespoons agave nectar

Directions:

1. Place all ingredients in a bowl and toss together.

2. For the dressing, combine the mayonnaise, agave, and mustard together in a separate bowl and mix well.

3. Top the salad with as much dressing as you like and enjoy!

19. SWEET AND SWEATY VEGAN CHILI

Ingredients:

- 2 Tbsp. high heat oil
- 1 chopped small yellow onion
- 2 chopped cloves of garlic
- 1 small can of crushed green chilies
- 2 cups vegan beef crumbles
- 1 tablespoon soy sauce
- 1 can tomato sauce
- 1 can petite diced tomatoes
- 1 tablespoon cumin
- 1/4 tablespoon pumpkin pie spice
- 1 teaspoon black pepper
- 1 tablespoon chili powder
- Soy sour cream (optional)
- Vegan shredded cheese (optional)

Directions:

1. In a large pot over medium-high heat, add garlic, green chilies, and onions and cook until the onions are translucent.

2. Add in the soy sauce and vegan beef crumbles and cook for about 5 minutes.

3. Then, add in the remaining ingredients, except the vegan dairy products, and stir until everything is mixed well. Allow to simmer for about 8 to 10 minutes after reducing heat. Continue to stir.

4.   Spoon into bowls and top with vegan cheese and sour cream, if you wish.

20. PUMPKIN RAVIOLI

Ingredients:

- 1 cup canned pumpkin purée
- 8 fresh vegan lasagna sheets
- 2 tablespoons vegan margarine
- 1/4 cup ground cashews
- Black pepper, to taste
- 1/2 teaspoon sea salt
- 1/4 teaspoon nutmeg
- 1/4 teaspoon cinnamon
- 1/4 teaspoons cumin

Directions:

1. In a small pan over medium heat, combine the margarine, cinnamon, nutmeg, pepper, salt, cumin, and cashews and cook over medium heat while stirring.

2. Then, add the pumpkin in and remain stirring until it reaches a mashed potato-like texture. Remove from heat.

3. Lay out the lasagna sheets flat and place a spoonful of the pumpkin mixture on each sheet about 2 inches apart. Place another sheet of lasagna on top and press down. Slice them into squares and seal the edges by pressing down with a fork.

4. Once the ravioli is sealed, add to water to boil them for roughly 10 to 15 minutes.

5.   Plate the ravioli and drizzle a sauce of your choice over top.

21. EASY VEGAN PESTO PIZZA

Ingredients:

- 1 cup vegan basil pesto
- 1/2 cup pine nuts
- 1/2 cup sundried tomatoes
- 8 small flour tortillas
- Olive oil

Directions:

1. Begin by preheating the oven to 350°F.

2. On each tortilla, spread pesto and top with a few sundried tomatoes and pine nuts.

3. Lay out the pizzas on a baking sheet and place in the oven for about 10 minutes.

4. Remove from the oven and drizzle with a little olive oil before cutting and serving.

22. VEGAN-STYLE REUBEN

Ingredients:

- 2 slices rye bread
- 1/2 an avocado
- 1/4 cup sauerkraut
- Mustard of your choice
- Thousand Island dressing

Directions:

1. On one bread slice, spread Thousand Island dressing and on the other slice, spread mustard.

2. Lay the bread slices in a lightly greased pan with the wet sides up. Top one of the slices of bread with sauerkraut and the other slice of bread with the avocado. Heat in the pan for a few minutes over medium heat.

3. Press the sandwich halves together and serve.

23. DILL PICNIC-STYLE VEGAN POTATO SALAD

Ingredients:

3 pounds peeled Yukon Gold potatoes
2 diced celery stalks
1 finely chopped red onion,
1 cup vegan mayonnaise
1 tablespoon lemon juice
1/4 cup chopped fresh dill
1 1/2 tablespoon apple cider vinegar
1 tablespoon Dijon mustard
Salt and Pepper, to taste

Directions:

1. In a large pot, add in peeled potatoes and boil for about 20 minutes. Season with salt.

2. Drain the potatoes and allow to cool.

3. In a large mixing bowl, combine all other ingredients and mix together well.

4. Once potatoes are cool, cut into small chunks and add them into the mixing bowl.

5. Stir together the potatoes and the other ingredients and refrigerate until ready to serve.

24. FRESH MANGO AND CUCUMBER SALAD

Ingredients:

- 1 bag baby spinach leaves, washed and drained
- 1 peeled mango, cut into small chunks
- 1 large peeled and sliced cucumber
- 1 cup sugar snap peas
- 1 diced red bell pepper
- 6 thinly sliced scallions
- 3 tablespoons lime Juice
- 1/2 cup seasoned rice vinegar
- Black pepper, to taste

Directions:

1. Place spinach into a large bowl.

2. Combine all other ingredients into another bowl and toss together. Then, pour over the spinach.

3. Top it off with more black pepper and enjoy!

25. COUSCOUS STUFFED PEPPERS

Ingredients:

- 1/2 cup couscous, prepare according to package instructions
- 1 cup boiling water
- 3 whole red bell peppers
- 3 whole yellow bell peppers
- 1/2 cup red bell peppers, diced
- 1/2 cup yellow bell peppers, diced
- 1/3 cup scallions, chopped
- 1/2 cup zucchini, diced
- 2 Tbsp. lime juice
- 2 Tbsp. olive oil
- 1/4 cup fresh dill, minced

Directions:

1. Prepare the couscous according to the package instructions and allow it to arrive at room temperature.

2. Slice off the tops of the whole bell peppers and remove the cores and seeds. Place on a plate and set aside.

3. Combine the remaining ingredients, except couscous, and mix together well.

4. Spoon the couscous into each pepper and top with other mixture.

5. Serve and enjoy!

Chapter 6: Desserts and Snacks Recipes

1. CARROT CAKE

Ingredients:

- 1 cup grated carrots;
- 1 cup shredded coconut;
- 1 cup Earth Balance spread;
- 1 cup pineapple, drained and crushed;
- 1 cup walnuts;
- 2 ½ teaspoons egg substitute, divided;
- 1/2 teaspoon salt;
- 2 ½ cups flour;
- 2 cups vegan dry sweetener;
- 2 teaspoons baking soda;
- 2 teaspoons cinnamon;
- 2 teaspoons vanilla; and
- 6 tablespoons water;

For your frosting:

- 1 container softened non-hydrogenated cream cheese;
- 1 cup liquid vegan sweetener;
- 1 teaspoon vanilla; and
- 1/4 cup Earth Balance spread.

Directions:

1. Line your baking pan with flour while preheating your oven to 325 degrees Fahrenheit.
2. Mix the egg substitute and water until it turns frothy. Set aside.

3. Mix the vegan sweetener and the Earth Balance until you arrive at a creamy mixture. Throw in the vanilla and egg replacer mixture and continue mixing. Set aside when done.
4. Mix the flour, baking soda, salt and cinnamon in another bowl. Add this mixture to the previous one.
5. Mix the pineapple and carrots in. Before transferring to the baking pan, fold the nuts and coconut into the mixture. Bake for up to 75 minutes in the preheated oven.
6. After baking, let the cake cool outside the oven before putting on a serving plate.
7. For the frosting, simply mix all frosting ingredients together until smooth. Spread on the cake and enjoy.

2. VEGAN SWEET TREAT

Ingredients:

- 1 1/3 cup dry vegan sweetener;
- 1 tablespoon cardamom;
- 1 tablespoon vanilla;
- 1/2 cup and another 2 tablespoons water;
- 1/2 cup Earth Balance Spread;
- 1/2 cup Tofutti Better Than Sour Cream;
- 1/2 teaspoon baking powder;
- 1/2 teaspoon salt;
- 2 ½ cups flour; and

3 ½ tablespoons of egg substitute, divided

For your topping:

- 1 cup pecans, chopped;
- 1/2 cup Earth Balance Spread; and
- 1/2 cup maple syrup.

Directions:

1. Line a baking pan with oil and flour while heating the oven to 325 degrees Fahrenheit.
2. Combine the flour, baking powder, cardamom and salt. Set aside.
3. Mix the egg substitute and water until frothy.
4. Cream the Earth Balance until fluffy in another bowl. Then, gradually mix in your vegan sweetener. Pour in the egg replacer mixture in five equal batches followed by the Tofutti and vanilla. Mix everything well.
5. Gradually mix in the dry ingredients into your mixture until fully combined.

6. Pour the batter in your baking pan and bake for up to an hour in your preheated oven. When done, let the cake cool outside the oven prior to putting it on your serving plate.
7. While baking, cook all the topping ingredients in medium-low heat.
8. Enjoy this delicious cake together with your prepared topping.

3. PETER PUMPKIN PARFAIT

Ingredients:

1 big pinch cinnamon;

1 cup vanilla soy yogurt;

1 small pinch nutmeg;

1 tablespoon maple syrup;

1 teaspoon vanilla extract; and

1/2 cup canned pumpkin puree (not pumpkin pie filling.)

Directions:

1. Mix together the cinnamon, maple syrup, nutmeg vanilla and pureed pumpkin.
2. Thoroughly whisk in the yogurt and refrigerate for at least an hour before enjoying chilled.

4. BASIL VINAIGRETTE FRUIT SALAD

Ingredients:

- Extra-virgin olive oil, 1 tablespoon;
- Fresh blueberries, 1 ½ cups;
- Fresh orange juice, 1 cup;
- Fresh strawberries, halved, 1 pound;
- Ripe peach, sliced into 16 wedges, 1 large piece;
- Salt;
- Small fresh basil leaves, 1/4 cup;
- Sugar, 1 ½ tablespoons; and
- White wine vinegar, 1 ½ tablespoons.

Directions:

1. Boil the sugar, orange juice and white wine in a small saucepan. Cook until the liquid is reduced to only half a cup. This should take around 15 minutes.
2. Whisk the oil and salt into the mixture. When done, allow mixture to stand for 2 minutes.
3. Combine the berries and peaches in a big bowl. Pour the juice mixture in and stir gently. Sprinkle basil over the mixture and enjoy.

5. FROZEN PEANUT BUTTER FUDGE TREATS

Ingredients:

- Coconut oil, melted, 2 tablespoons;
- Honey, 2 tablespoons;
- Peanut butter, 1/2 cup;
- Salt, ¼ teaspoon; and
- Vanilla extract, 1/4 teaspoon.

Directions:

1. Add all the ingredients together in a mixing bowl. Mix until everything's combined well. If it proves difficult to mix, microwave for up to 15 seconds.
2. Pour the fudge on the plastic wrap or parchment paper-lined container. You may use a regular loaf pan or a simple plastic container.
3. Leave the container in the freezer for up to 40 minutes to let the fudge set. After hardening completely, remove the fudge from the freezer and let it sit for 5 minutes in room temperature.
4. Carefully cut up your fudge into 8 squares with a sharp knife. Store them in a plastic container or plastic bag in the freezer until you're ready to devour them.

6. YOUR FAVORITE NON-DAIRY CHOCOLATE PUDDING

Ingredients:

- Cornstarch, 3 tablespoons;
- Soy milk, 1 ½ cups;
- Unsweetened cocoa powder, 1/4 cup;
- Vanilla extract, ¼ teaspoon;
- Water, 2 tablespoons; and
- White sugar, ¼ cup.

Directions:

1. Create a paste by mixing the corn starch and water in a small bowl. Bring this mixture – along with the sugar, cocoa, vanilla, and soy milk – to a boil over medium heat. Stir frequently.
2. Once it boils, continue stirring frequently and cooking until it becomes thick. Then, remove the pudding from heat and cool for up to 5 minutes.
3. Place the pudding in the fridge to cool completely before enjoying.

7. SANGRIA SHAVED ICE

Ingredients:

- 100% Concord grape juice, 1 cup;
- Fruity red wine, 1 ¾ cups;
- Lemon rind, finely grated, 1 teaspoon;
- Orange rind, finely grated, 2 teaspoons; and
- Sugar, 1/8 – 1/4 cup.

Directions:

1. Boil the sugar and juice together in a small saucepan over medium high heat. Do this for about 1 minute, staring continuously to completely dissolve the sugar. Remove saucepan from heat once finished.
2. Mix the rinds in and allow the mixture to completely cool at room temperature. When done, use a fine sieve to strain the mixture into a clean bowl, removing solid particles. Mix the wine in and thoroughly combine by stirring.
3. In an 11-inch baking dish, pour in the mixture and cover before leaving inside the freezer for up to 5 hours, scraping everything every 45 minutes until completely frozen.
4. When done, removed from the freezer and scrape all until fluffy.

8. VEGAN COOKIE BITES

Ingredients:

- Agave nectar, 1 tablespoon;
- Almond butter, 4 tablespoons;
- Baking soda, 1/8 teaspoon;
- Chickpeas, rinsed and drained, 1 ½ cups;
- Cinnamon, 1 to 2 teaspoons;
- Coconut oil, 2 tablespoons;
- Ginger, 1 ½ teaspoons;
- Molasses, 2 tablespoons;
- Raisins, 1/3 cup;
- Salt to taste;
- Semi-sweet vegan chocolate chips, ¾ cup;
- Uncooked oats, ½ cup; and
- Vanilla extract, 1 tablespoon.

Directions:

1. Use a food processor or blender to blend together the chickpeas, agave nectar, molasses, vanilla, almond butter, spices, baking soda and salt until you get a smooth consistency. Pour all of the mixture into a medium-sized bowl.
2. Form the dough by mixing in the oats, 1/3 cup of the raisins and 1/3 cup of semi-sweet vegan chocolate chips. Make 32 small balls from the dough and place them on a baking sheet lined with tin foil. Freeze the balls in the freezer for up to 15 minutes to harden.
3. While freezing the balls, melt the remaining chocolate and coconut oil by microwaving in a microwave safe bowl in 20-second intervals until you get a smooth consistency. Stir the mixture after each interval.

4. Take out the balls from the freezer and dip each of them in the melted mixture of oil and chocolate. Put them back on the baking sheet and return to the freezer to harden further.

5. After hardening, let the balls thaw for several minutes after taking out from the freezer and before enjoying the treats.

9. VEGAN CUPCAKES

Ingredients:

All purpose flour, 2 cups;

Almond milk, 1 1/2 cups;

Apple cider vinegar, 1 tablespoon;

Baking powder, 2 teaspoons;

Baking soda, ½ teaspoon;

Coconut oil, warmed to liquid, ½ cup;

Salt, ½ teaspoon;

Vanilla extract, 1 ¼ teaspoons; and

White sugar, 1 cup.

Directions:

1. Grease 2 muffin pans that can hold 12 cups while heating your oven to 350 degrees Fahrenheit.
2. Mix 1 ½ cups almond milk with a tablespoon of the vinegar. Allow to curdle by letting it stand for 5 minutes.
3. Whisk the baking soda, sugar, salt, baking powder and flour in a big mixing bowl.
4. Mix the almond milk mixture, vanilla extract and coconut oil in another bowl before mixing with the dry ingredients mixture earlier mentioned. Stir until well-combined.
5. Fill the cups of your muffin pans with the mixture and bake in the preheated oven for up to 20 minutes or until cupcakes bounce back after pushed down lightly.
6. Allow the muffins to cool on a wire rack after baking. Add your choice frosting, if desired.

10. OAT-CHIA COOKIES

Ingredients:

- Applesauce, 2/3 cup;
- Baking powder, ½ teaspoon;
- Baking soda, 1 teaspoon;
- Brown sugar, 1 cup;
- Chia seeds, 2 tablespoons;
- Coconut oil, 3 tablespoons;
- Dried cranberries, 1 cup;
- Ground cinnamon, 1 teaspoon;
- Rolled oats, 2 cups;
- Salt, ½ teaspoon;
- Unsweetened shredded coconut ¼ cup; and
- Whole-wheat flour, 2/3 cup.

Directions:

1. Line a baking sheet with parchment paper while preheating your oven to 350 degrees Fahrenheit.
2. Mix the baking powder, salt, cinnamon, baking soda, flour, chia seeds, oats and brown sugar in a medium-sized bowl followed by the applesauce and coconut oil. Mix until you get an evenly mixed dough.
3. Fold the cranberries and shredded coconuts into your dough. Spoon 12 cookies onto the baking sheet and bake in the preheated oven for up to 15 minutes or until the edges of the cookies become lightly browned. Let them cool before enjoying.

11. VEGAN GINGER COOKIES

Ingredients:

- All-purpose flour, 1 ½ cups;
- Applesauce, 1/2 cup;
- Baking powder, 1 teaspoon;
- Baking soda, ½ teaspoon;
- Cooking spray;
- Crystallized ginger, chopped, ¾ cup;
- Ginger, ground, ½ teaspoon;
- Lemon juice, 1 tablespoon;
- Lemon rind, grated, 1 teaspoon;
- Salt, ½ teaspoon;
- Sugar, 1 ¼ cup divided;
- Vanilla extract, 1/4 teaspoon;
- Vegetable oil, 1/4 cup; and
- Whole wheat flour, 1 cup.

Directions:

Pour the flours into your dry measuring cups and level each using a knife. Mix the crystallized ginger, flours, baking soda, baking powder, ground ginger and salt and whisk to stir well. When done, create a hole at the center of the mixture.

Mix the vegetable oil, applesauce, lemon juice, lemon rind, a cup of sugar and vanilla extract well and pour this in the hole at the center your earlier flour mixture. Mix well to get a moist dough.

Chill the dough for 1 hour with cover. Preheat oven to 350 degrees Fahrenheit while doing so.

Coat your hands lightly with flour and make 24 balls from your dough. Roll each in sugar and arrange them about 2 inches apart on baking sheets coated with cooking spray.

Bake the balls in the oven for up to 15 minutes or until light brown in color. Cool the balls in the pan for 1 minute when done. Then, transfer on wire racks to cool completely.

12. VEGAN CHOCOLATE COOKIES

Ingredients:

For cookie rolling

- Granulated sugar, ¼ cup; and
- Powdered sugar, 1 cup.

For the cookie dough

- All-purpose flour, 1 ¼ cups and 2 tablespoons;
- Baking powder, ¾ tablespoons;
- Canola oil, 1/3 cup;
- Dark corn syrup, 2 tablespoons;
- Ground flax seeds, 1 tablespoon;
- Natural cocoa powder, 2 tablespoons;
- Pure vanilla extract, 1 teaspoon;
- Salt, ¼ teaspoon;
- Soy milk, 1/3 cup;
- Sugar, ¾ cup; and
- Vegan chocolate chips, melted, ½ cup.

Directions:

1. While preheating oven to 325 degrees Fahrenheit, pour ¼ cup granulated sugar in a small bowl. In another bowl, sift ½ cup powdered sugar. Set aside both sugars for rolling the cookies in later.
2. Melt the chocolate in a microwavable bowl by microwaving in 30-second intervals. In between intervals, stir the chocolate to smoothen.
3. In a big mixing bowl, combine the flax seeds, melted chocolates, vanilla, soymilk, oil, dark corn syrup and sugar. Mix until smooth.

4. Sift the baking powder, salt, flour and cocoa powder into the earlier smooth mixture and stir until the dough becomes thick and moist.

5. Leave the dough in the fridge for up to 20 minutes and when done, make approximately 24 cookie balls, each from a tablespoon's worth of the dough, and roll them on the granulated sugar first then the powdered one.

6. Arrange your cookies on baking sheets lined with parchment paper then bake in the preheated oven for about 14 minutes.

7. After baking, allow to cool for 5 minutes on the baking sheets before cooling on the wire rack completely.

13. CHOCOLATE COCONUT ALMOND BARS

Ingredients:

For The Topping:

- 1/2 cup vegan chocolate chips;
- 1/2 tablespoon virgin coconut oil;
- 1/4 cup shredded unsweetened coconut; and
- 1/4 cup toasted unsweetened large coconut flakes.

For The Base:

- 1 cup gluten-free rolled oats.
- 3/4 cup whole almonds;
- 1/4 cup virgin coconut oil -3 tablespoons pure maple syrup;
- 1/2 cup gluten-free oat flour;
- 1/4 teaspoon fine grain sea salt; and

For The Middle Layer:

- 1 cup raw or roasted almond butter;
- 1/2 cup virgin coconut oil;
- 1/4 cup maple syrup;
- 1/2 cup rice cereal.
- 1/2 tablespoon pure vanilla extract
- pinch of fine grain sea salt; and

Directions:

1. Line your 8-inch square pan with 2 parchment papers while preheating your oven to 350 degrees Fahrenheit. **For The Crust:**
2. Process the almonds in your processor until it becomes fine meal – smaller than sand.

3. Make oat flour by processing the oats until it becomes flour-like in texture.
4. Mix in the almond meal, oil, oat flour, salt and syrup and process some more until sticky and combined. Finally, mix the rolled oats in and continue processing until your dough comes together and the oats have been chopped. When pressed with your fingers, the dough should stick together.
5. Evenly crumble your dough in the lined pan and press it evenly into the pan. Wet your fingers to avoid sticking.
6. Use a pastry roller to smooth out your dough and press the edges even with your fingertips.
7. After poking a few holes to release air, bake in the preheated oven for up to 13 minutes without cover. Let the pan cool on the cooling rack for 10 minutes afterwards.
8. Heat together the oil, almond butter, vanilla, syrup and salt over medium heat until the oil has melted and you get a smooth mixture. Whisk if needed before removing from heat.
9. When the crust has cooled, mix the rice crisp cereal with the almond butter mixture. Top the cooled crust with this mixture and smoothen it out. Leave it in the freezer for up to 45 minutes or until the middle layer completely solidifies.
10. Toast your coconut flakes while freezing the mixture. Do this by toasting the flakes at 350 degrees Fahrenheit for up to 4 minutes only or until golden. Allow to cool before breaking flakes into smaller crumbs to sprinkle easily later on.
11. Once the middle layer's completely frozen, take it out of the freezer and lift the bar out. Slice the bars into 6 vertical rows and 3 horizontal rows to get 18 bars. Put

them back in the freezer while you make the chocolate topping.

For the chocolate topping:

12. Melt the coconut oil and chocolate together in a saucepan in low-medium heat. Once half of the chocolate chips have melted, stir away from heat until completely smooth.

14. Stir the shredded coconut in.

To Assemble:

15. Take the bars from the freezer and top each with a small amount of the chocolate topping. Sprinkle immediately with the coconut flakes before returning to the freezer to completely set the chocolate.

14. MUSCLE POWER SEED BITES

Ingredients:

- 1 cup packed pitted dates;
- 1/4 cup hulled hemp seed;
- 1/4 cup chia seed;
- 1/4 cup sesame seed;
- 1/4 cup cocoa powder;
- 1/2 teaspoon pure vanilla extract;
- 1/4 teaspoon cinnamon;
- 1/4 teaspoon fine grain sea salt, or to taste; and
- 1/4 cup raw cocoa nibs.

Directions:

1. In a food processor, blend the dates to create a chunky paste.
2. Mix the chia, hemp, cocoa, sesame, cinnamon, vanilla and salt in. Blend until everything's combined. Pulse the cacao nibs in to get a dough, which should be sticky when you use your fingers to press it. If it is not sticky enough for rounding up into balls, add some water and blend again until it becomes sticky enough.
3. Make about 16 small balls and freeze for 20 minutes to firm up.
4. Enjoy or store the excess in the fridge for future snack attacks!

15. EASY-PEASY NO-BAKE CHOCOROONS

Ingredients:

- 1 finely mashed banana;
- 1/4 cup pure maple syrup;
- 1/4 cup melted coconut oil;
- 1/2 tsp. pure vanilla extract;
- 6 tbsp. cocoa powder, sifted;
- 1 ½ cups unsweetened shredded coconut; and
- A pinch of fine grain sea salt, to taste.

Directions:

1. Mash banana in a medium-sized bowl until no more clumps. Mix the maple syrup, melted coconut oil and vanilla in.
2. Sift cocoa powder into the mix and stir to combine well.
3. Mix the coconut and salt in and stir to combine.
4. Use a non-stick mat or parchment paper to line your baking sheet. Scoop rounds of the mixture onto it using a spoon and leave the sheet in the freezer for 20 minutes or until they firm up.
5. Enjoy cold or softened at room temperature.

16. PB&J ROLLS

Ingredients:

Rolls

- 4 slices white bread, crust removed
- 4 tablespoons natural vegan peanut butter
- 4 Tablespoons jam of your choice

Raspberry Sauce (to dip)

- 2 tablespoons raspberry vinegar
- 1 tablespoon balsamic vinegar
- dash vegan Worcestershire sauce
- 1/2 teaspoon chopped and peeled shallots
- 2 tablespoons sugar
- 1 peeled garlic clove
- pinch dried basil
- pinch dried oregano
- 1 cup fresh raspberries
- 1 cup olive oil

Directions:

1. Roll out each piece of white bread until they are flat. Spread the jelly and peanut butter over the pieces of bread. Then, roll up the bread as if you were rolling up sushi and cut, horizontally, into pieces. Set aside.
2. Add the dipping sauce ingredients into your blender or food processor and place lid on top. Blend until well mixed and serve with the rolls to dip.

17. RASPBERRY BANANA SMOOTHIE

Ingredients:

- 1 cup vegan almond milk
- 1 cup fresh spinach
- 1/2 cup chopped romaine
- 1/4 cup mint leaves
- 2 peeled ripe bananas
- 1 1/2 cups raspberries (frozen)

Directions:

1. Add all of the ingredients into your blender and blend until smooth. Drink up!

18. SUMMER PEACH SORBET

Ingredients:

- 3 fresh peaches
- 1/2 teaspoon vanilla extract
- 3/4 cup sugar
- 4 cups ice cubes

Directions:

1. Add all of the ingredients into your blender or food processor.
2. Pulsate on low and gradually increase speed for 40 seconds.
3. Serve right away.

19. GRANDMA'S APPLE PIE ICE CREAM

Ingredients:

- 3 ounces frozen apple juice concentrate
- 1/4 cup vanilla soy yogurt
- 1/2 cored apple
- 1 tablespoon vanilla extract
- 1/4 teaspoon cinnamon
- 1/2 a peeled ripe banana
- 3 cups ice cubes

Directions:

1. Add all of the ingredients into your blender or food processor.
2. Pulsate on low and gradually increase speed for 30 seconds.
3. Serve right away.

20. HOMEMADE STRAWBERRY CHIA JAM

Ingredients:

- 1 pound fresh strawberries (green stems removed)
- 1/4 cup sweet apple cider vinegar
- 2 tablespoons agave
- 1 seeded serrano pepper
- 2 tablespoons chia seeds

Directions:

1. Add all of the ingredients into your blender or food processor.
2. Pulsate on low and gradually increase speed for 40 seconds.
3. Serve right away or refrigerate for later. Great for breakfast and snacks, too.

Chapter 7: Sample 4-Week Diet Plan

An important part of living a healthy and successful vegan lifestyle is to plan ahead. This sample 4-week diet plan will give you an example of how you can incorporate some of the aforementioned recipes into a weekly meal plan that will help you stay on track while transitioning to veganism. You can alter or swap out any of the recipes with another of your choice to make it work better for you and your taste buds! Just make sure to keep it vegan!

Week 1				
	Breakfast	Lunch	Dinner	Dessert/ Snacks
Monday	Tofu Breakfast Delight	Veggie Sauté	Salad Con Mexico	Carrot Cake For Vegans
Tuesday	Morning Tortillas	Black Bean Burger	The Popeye Salad	Vegan Sweet Treat
Wed	It's A Parfait Day	Veggie Soy Stir-fry	Fruit Salad	Peter Pumpkin Parfait
Thursday	ChickPea pper Cake	Coco Sauté	Chili Pesto Beans	Basil Vinaigrette Fruit Salad

Friday	A Different Kind Of Porridge	Green Quinoa Curry	Mango Veggie Spice Salad	Frozen Peanut Butter Treats
Saturday	Las Migans	Vegan Casserole	Avocado Sandwich	Your Fav. Non-Dairy Chocolate Pudding
Sunday	Fried Brekkie Potatoes	Sweet Potato Bakes	Avocado-bean Club Sandwich	Sangria Shaved Ice

		Breakfast	Lunch	Dinner	Dessert/Snacks
Week 2					
		Breakfast	Lunch	Dinner	Dessert/Snacks
Monday		DIY Vegan Hazelnut Spread And Bread	Vurrito Bowl	Pizzuchinis	Vegan Chocolate Cookie Bites
Tuesday		A Berry Blue Oatmeal Waffle	Mushroom Pepperjitas	The Green Caper Linguine	Vegan cupcakes
Wed		Muffins with Jelly	Vegan-wich	Almond Roast Pepper Pasta	Oat-Chia Cookies
Thursday		Tofumelet	Veggie Sauté	Stephen's Curried Eggplant, Basil And Tomato	Vegan Ginger Cookies
Friday		Bean & Avocado Toast	Vegetables Soy	Quinoatato Salad	Vegan Chocolate Cookies
Saturday		Banana Vegan Bread	Green Quinoa Curry	The Ultimate Veggie Burger	Chocolate Coconut Almond Bars
Sunday		Vegan Quiche	Sweet Potato Bakes	Vegan Soup Delight	Muscle Power Seed Bites

Week 3

	Breakfast	Lunch	Dinner	Dessert/Snacks
Monday	Warm Nutty Cinnamon Quinoa	Vurrito Bowl	Lentil Squash Soup	No-Bake Chocoroons
Tuesday	Morning Tortillas	Vegan-wich	Salad Con Mexico	Carrot Cake For Vegans
Wed	ChickPeapper Cake	Burger Of Beans	Fruit Salad	Peter Pumpkin Parfait
Thursday	Las Migans	Coco Sauté	Mango Veggie Spice Salad	Frozen Peanut Butter Fudge Treats
Friday	DIY Vegan Hazelnut Spread and Bread	Vegan Casserole	Avocado-bean Club Sandwich	Vegan Chocolate Cookie Bites
Saturday	Muffins with Jelly	Mushroom Pepperjitas	The Green Caper Linguine	Oat-Chia Cookies
Sunday	Bean & Avocado Toast	Green Quinoa Curry	Stephen's Curried Eggplant	Vegan Chocolate Cookies

Week 4

	Breakfast	Lunch	Dinner	Dessert/Snacks
Monday	Vegan Quiche	Veggie Sauté	The Ultimate Veggie Burger	Muscle Power Seed Bites
Tuesday	Tofu Breakfast Delight	Vegetables Soy	Lentil Squash Soup	Vegan Sweet Treat
Wed	It's A Parfait Day	Sweet Potato Bake	The Popeye Salad	Basil Fruits Vinaigrette
Thursday	A Different Kind Of Porridge	Black Bean Burger	Chili Pesto Beans	Milk-Less Choco Pudding
Friday	Fried Brekkie Potatoes	Green Quinoa Curry	Avocado Pea Sandwich	Vegan Cupcakes
Saturday	A Berry Blue Oatmeal Waffle	Vurrito Bowl	Pizzuchinis	Vegan Ginger Cookies
Sunday	Tofumelet	Vegan-wich	Almond Roasted Pepper Pasta	Chocolate Coconut Almond Bars

Chapter 8: Tips for Beginners

Your vegan journey is one that can lead you to great health and vitality; but it is not necessarily an easy one to start. If you're used to eating meat your whole life, here are 16 tips to help you successfully transition into a life of great vegan bliss.

1. **First things first, you need to be open-minded**. The best way to fail in your vegan journey, before you have even started, is to begin with a negative attitude. If you're open to the possibility that you can actually live without meat, then half the battle is already won; but, if you feel like switching to a vegan diet is a punishment or a chore, than you will likely not succeed. You have to *want* to become a vegan and be open to the chance that this really could be a good thing for you.

2. **Give yourself enough time to cook meals at home and pre-make meals to bring to work for breakfast and lunch**. This is especially important as a beginner vegan, because it can be quite difficult to stay on a vegan diet if you don't prepare your own food. Since most commercially available foods, whether it is in the supermarket or restaurants, use meat or many ingredients that are derived from animals, not bringing your own food can make it really difficult, if not impossible, for you to stay vegan. Considering that food preparation can take some time, the wise thing to do as a beginner is to give yourself ample time for preparing meals ahead of time. It will be easier for you in the long run. It helps to even set aside one night a week, such as a Sunday night, to prepare your meals for the week and freeze them. This will add to the convenience of grabbing a home-cooked meal right from your freezer to enjoy later in the day.

3. **Avoid consuming convenience foods from the local gas station/deli or grocery store.** Chances are, most commercially produced vegan food that you can get at the supermarket or convenience store, assuming they even have those, are likely loaded with preservative and sodium, and don't taste as good as those that you can prepare at home. If you always choose convenience foods over a home-cooked meal, your palate will easily get tired and bored to the point that you may quit being vegan altogether.

4. **Evaluate the contents of your pantry.** You have likely been a carnivore all your life and chances are, your pantry or freezer is stocked with of meat products or condiments that are either meat-based or contain ingredients that are derived from animals. In starting your vegan journey, it is best to clear your pantry of any possible source of temptation and replace them with vegan-friendly alternatives. Instead of throwing out the non-vegan, non-perishable food items, donate them to a local food bank so that the less fortunate can benefit from your transition, as well!

5. **You will need to really familiarize yourself with your grocery store's produce section.** Starting your journey is the single best excuse to become passionate about the fruits and vegetables you hardly ever ate when you were still a carnivore. By familiarizing yourself with such, you'll be able to significantly widen your choices for vegan eating and ensure that your palate never gets bored or dull. Try things you have never had before, because you might be surprised that you actually really like it. Being a vegan is enjoyable as you make it out to be, so don't be afraid to branch out and try something new! Also, make sure you are buying the freshest produce you can buy and don't buy more than you plan to eat. It will only go bad before you can eat it and no one likes to waste food or money.

6. **Don't forget to plan ahead.** Failing to plan ahead is practically the equivalent to planning for failure when it comes to living a vegan lifestyle. As mentioned earlier, lack of commercially available and delicious vegan foods can really be a disaster. The only way to avoid such a risk is to plan ahead. If you need to, pack a day's worth of meals to ensure that you stay on track. This is especially important if you are going on a trip and won't necessarily have access to any vegan options. Even an apple or some trail mix will help you in those sticky situations. Keep vegan snacks in your desk at work or a pre-made meal in your office's freezer. That way, in case you forget your lunch, you won't have to worry about having nothing to eat or spending too much on dining out. You will thank yourself later.

7. **Don't be too hard on yourself.** So what if you make mistakes? Going vegan isn't an easy task and for most people, it is trial and error until you get the hang of it. Considering that you have a lifetime's worth of dependence, or even addiction, to meat and its byproducts, it is normal to slip up or slide back into eating meat every once in a while at the beginning. The important thing is to learn from your mistakes and to forgive yourself because you're only human. Just stay the course and in due time, you'll be pleasantly surprised to find that you no longer crave meat and other non-vegan foods that you once were dependent on. Remember, show the same compassion for yourself as you do with animals.

8. **Never look down on someone for their lifestyle choices.** Once you have gotten the hang of being a vegan, be conscious of how you treat others who do not live a vegan lifestyle. Remember the phrase, "To each their own," as not everyone has to have the same views and lifestyle choices as you do. You should also remember that you were once in their place and it was your choice along to transition into being

vegan. Don't lecture your friends and family about becoming vegan; but instead, cook up a delicious vegan entrée or side to bring to the next dinner party or picnic you are invited to. You'll likely end up *impressing* them, rather than *pressuring* them.

9. **Make it a weekly event to go to the farmer's market.** Grab a friend or your significant other and make a day out of checking out your local farmer's market. It is fun to walk around and browse all the locally grown fruits, vegetables, and herbs, as well as the homemade jams, breads, and treats that will compliment your vegan diet perfectly. You'll find it entertaining and exciting to go to a place where *nearly everything* is vegan friendly, for a change!

10. **Dine out for a change.** Although we stress the importance of cooking at home, it is important to treat yourself to a meal cooked by someone else every so often. There are many vegan restaurants and bakeries that will allow you to get out of the house, without getting off track of your vegan diet. The plus side to this is that you may get new ideas for meals to try making at home, too!

11. **It's easy to not be cheesy.** For some people, giving up cheese is the only obstacle standing between being a vegetarian and being a vegan. It seems as if everything these days is topped, stuffed, or layered with cheeses of all kind. It may seem impossible to go without this ingredient that is a staple in most people's homes, and mouths. Don't stress, though! There are plenty of alternatives for cheese, as well as vegan-friendly cheeses that you can curb your cravings with.

12. **Spice up your life.** One of the many misconceptions about veganism is that the cuisine is bland and boring. As you have read in the recipes in this book, adding the right spices to your meals can really make a difference and can turn an

"okay" meal into a delicious one that you will want to make over and over again. Many spices, such as cumin and curry, are often added to vegan meals to boost them with flavor. In addition to spices, adding fresh cilantro, dill, or basil to your entrée can really make your meal pop. Don't forget the Sriracha, too!

13. **Educate yourself in order to stay motivated.** Reading this book is a very important first step towards educating yourself on what veganism is all about and how you can easily incorporate it into your daily life. It can be easy to fall off track, but if you feel tempted to stray from veganism, pick up a book or watch a documentary about the inhumane and disgusting ways that animals are slaughtered and prepared for "food." You will surely lose your appetite for meat. Also, take a trip to your local farm or animal sanctuary and befriend the animals. You'll find it very difficult to eat them after that.

14. **Connect with the vegan community.** Whether it is following blogs or your favorite vegans on Instagram, or joining a local group – getting involved with fellow vegans will help you stay on track and allow you to branch out when it comes to foods and the vegan way of life.

15. **Ease into your transition into veganism.** Instead of going "cold turkey," pardon that phrase, with your dietary transition, try swapping out one item a week for a vegan option. For example, try to swap out meat with just veggies or a veggie or black bean burger, instead of a hamburger. Making small changes instead of cutting out everything all together will make your transition into becoming a vegan much easier. You'll find that you will begin to prefer these alternatives to the foods you once loved and you won't feel like you are "punishing" yourself for cutting them out of your diet.

16. **How to Shop Vegan on a Budget.** One of the biggest obstacles beginner vegans have when transitioning to the vegan lifestyle is that some organic foods and vegan alternatives are more expensive than non-vegan foods. While this may be true for some products, there are many ways to make eating vegan affordable and generally inexpensive. As mentioned before, it's important to plan ahead. Write out your meals for the week and write a separate list of the ingredients that you will need for each meal. It's easier to choose meals that have similar ingredients so that you have less to buy. When you go to the grocery store, make sure that you only buy what you have written down on your list. This will prevent you from purchasing unnecessary extra food items that will increase your grocery bill. Don't forget to compare prices between grocery stores and also between name brand and generic brand items. Consider the price differences in frozen fruits compared to fresh, and see how they add up. Sometimes it's better to buy frozen fruits when they are not in season. Out of season fresh fruits are often more expensive and less pricey than when in season.

Also, try shopping at stores like Costco and Sam's club, where you can purchase bulk sizes of items that you use a lot of; such as, beans, vegan pastas, spices, etc. Although it may seem like more money up front, you will be spending less money in the long run.

When making dinners, try to make enough so that you have leftovers for the next day. Most soups and pasta dishes that you make in excess can be frozen and heated up for another day. This will save you time if you are running late and need a quick, but healthy, meal. Having extra meals around will also prevent you from eating out as much. Although dining out is perfectly acceptable every now and then, it can really add up if you are doing it several times a week.

So, contrary to popular belief, eating healthy and vegan is not more expensive than eating non-vegan. In fact, it can even be less expensive due to the rising costs of meats and meat bi-products. You could buy ingredients for 3 or more meals for the same price as a pound of ground beef.

Conclusion:

Thank you again for purchasing this book and congratulations on finishing it! You should now be ready to put your unhealthy life behind you and begin your journey to a healthy vegan lifestyle. As you have read, the two most important parts of being successful as a vegan are, educating yourself and putting your plan into action. Living a vegan lifestyle doesn't have to be hard and it doesn't have to be expensive either.

I encourage you to try out at least one recipe each for breakfast, lunch, dinner and desserts and snacks and proceed from there. Taking small steps is much better than taking none at all. Remember, it is easy to get back on track if you slip up, so don't be discouraged! I'm confident that as you taste these delicious recipes, you'll be encouraged to go vegan all the way!

Here's to your health!

Best wishes,

Jenny Walker

Don't forget to turn the page to get my FREE BONUS GIFTS just for you!

Here's your exclusive FREE BONUS!

Want FREE & 99c Kindle book deals sent straight to your inbox every week? Save money on books and read more!

I'm able to give you free, exclusive access to my publisher's book club, the **Epic Kindle Deals Book Club**. Here's what you get when you join:

- **FREE** and **99c** nonfiction books every week on healthy living, diets, recipe books, fitness, and self-improvement!
- Save money: Never pay more than 99c for a book ever again!
- Random Amazon gift giveaways

This exclusive offer won't last forever, so **go to the URL below** to claim your spot and join now.

http://bit.ly/1PRXxhC

BONUS CHAPTER:

I want to share a FREE chapter with you, from my other vegan book, which focuses on how to make *high protein* vegan recipes. I think you might like it as well! It contains even more great-tasting recipes...

Chapter from *"Vegan: The High Protein Vegan Cookbook: Eat Vegan & Still Get the Protein You Need"*:

As we have seen, one of the issues people have with becoming a vegan is that they may not get enough protein in their diet. But there are other ways of introducing protein into your diet, even if you do not eat meat. There are some vegan high protein meal options that can give you the best of both worlds; you can be a vegan and greatly reduce the fat and calories you take in, all while still getting enough lean protein into your system so you can keep your lean muscle mass.

While it certainly is not impossible to get enough protein, zinc and B12 into your diet if you cut out all animal by products such as meat, eggs, cheese and milk, it will be a little more challenging to do so. As long as you are aware of the need to keep vegan high protein alternatives around and introduce them into your daily diet, it should all work out just fine.

Of course, one easy way to get these vitamins and minerals into your daily diet is to take a full spectrum multi vitamin. There are many on the market and some are better than others. In a lot of cases, so I have been told, the liquid nutritional supplements are better than the pills because they are absorbed more easily. I don't know if that is true, talk to your doctor to make sure. Either way, introducing a quality multi vitamin into your daily diet can't be a bad thing.

There are more and more vegetarian and vegan products on the market all the time. I'd bet your nearest health foods store will have a full line of vegan and vegetarian foods. Just go look around your nearest organic store and you will be amazed at your options for plant-based protein.

Along with some of the brands of organic and vegan foods you can get at your local organic store, you also have a wide variety of raw foods from which to choose. Great sources of protein are beans. All kinds of beans but especially kidney and garbanzo beans. Black beans are also loaded with protein and they can make a wild chile!

Many kinds of nuts can really pack a lot of protein into a small size. Almonds, pecans, walnuts, pistachios and cashews are a great high protein snack. And since you can eat them raw, they are easy and quick too.

As I hope I have illustrated, even though you do need to keep a close eye on your nutritional needs if you are a vegan or vegetarian, there are many ways to ensure that you get all the vegan high protein into your diet that you need. Whether you opt for a supplement or you choose to add some nuts to your daily snacks, or both, you can keep your lean muscle mass while still lowering your intake of saturated fat and cholesterol.

Here are some ingredients you can look for at the store which are great vegan protein sources:

Lentils
Tofu
Black Beans
Quinoa
Amaranth
Green Peas
Hemp seeds (you can put these in smoothies!)
Oatmeal
Artichokes
Pumpkin seeds
Hemp milk
Broccoli
Almonds
Spirulina
Chickpeas

There are more options too, but this should be enough to get you started. Feel free to substitute/add these ingredients into the recipes in this book!

Want to read more? This book contains even more delicious vegan high protein recipes! Grab the book now on Amazon here: http://amzn.to/1VXd2wU

Did you like this book?

If you liked this book (or if you didn't), I'd love to hear your feedback and if it helped you. I welcome all feedback and use it to make my books better, so please go here to leave a review: **http://amzn.to/1TDiPl8**

Printed in Great Britain
by Amazon